A LOVE LETTER TO EUROPE

A LOVE LETTER TO EUROPE

*An outpouring of sadness
and hope from writers,
thinkers and artists*

CORONET

First published in Great Britain in 2019 by Coronet
An Imprint of Hodder & Stoughton
An Hachette UK company

1

Compilation © Hodder & Stoughton Limited
Essays © individual authors

A CIP catalogue record for this title is available from the British Library

Hardback ISBN 978 1 529 38110 8
eBook ISBN 978 1 529 38109 2

Typeset in Sabon MT by Hewer Text UK Ltd, Edinburgh
Printed and bound in Great Britain by Clays Ltd, Elcograf S.p.A.

Hodder & Stoughton policy is to use papers that are natural, renewable
and recyclable products and made from wood grown in sustainable
forests. The logging and manufacturing processes are expected to
conform to the environmental regulations of the country of origin.

Hodder & Stoughton Ltd
Carmelite House
50 Victoria Embankment
London EC4Y 0DZ

www.hodder.co.uk

CONTENTS

Love at first sight

Let me count the ways

Come live with me

Opening the door a little wider

My North, my South, my East and West

If music be the food of love

Angoisse des gares

Reckless with others' hearts

The love you take

PUBLISHER'S INTRODUCTION

The idea for this book crystallised in the last week of July 2019 when a new Prime Minister came to power declaring that Britain would leave the EU on 31 October 'no ifs no buts'. This declaration did nothing to decrease uncertainty around Brexit.

We are living through a turning point in our history and whatever happens, Britain's relations with Europe will be more confused, more troubled. Many Brits feel increasingly anxious and not a little powerless.

With so many negotiating positions and so much posturing, public discourse seems to many to have become completely detached from our hopes and fears. This has been made more disturbing by various agencies' attempts to subvert the distinction between true and false.

In the face of all this uncertainty, is there anything we can be sure of?

Something we *can* be sure of is what we feel, our subjective experience. Great writers are often adept at capturing this on the page, tracking directions of the heart, its dramatic turns and subtle shifts. Such writers also have a way of finding something holy in the heart's affections. And some of the greatest writers can delineate with precision how turning points in history reverberate in the innermost depths. When a new kind of sadness comes into the world – or a new kind of tenderness – they know it.

Could a book be a place for writers to affirm a collective love for Europe? Could it perhaps be a keepsake like love letters, a sort of totem of vivid, authentic feelings?

Britain has an extraordinarily rich and diverse culture – impossible to represent fully in a few hundred pages – but we decided to try to unite as many different voices as possible in a harmonious chorus or outpouring. In August we began to approach creative people of different ages, ethnicities and orientations. We asked novelists, artists, musicians, science fiction writers, nature writers, travel writers, broadcasters, humourists, historians, scientists, actors, cooks, explorers, an English woman who set up and runs a vineyard in France, an author who is a four-star general, another is a former diplomat who remembers Vienna as 'the playground of spies', another is a school principal, another works in refugee camps.

This is from the email we sent:

On 31 October we are publishing a book called *A Love Letter to Europe*. We don't know what will happen on that day, but it will probably be sad and a cause for continuing anxiety.

We want this book to be an affirmation, a chorus of love for Europe. We do love you. We still love you.

The idea, then, is to ask British writers and thinkers to say what they love about Europe as a whole or, perhaps more likely, something big or small they found to love about a particular European country. We're not looking for anything overtly political. We're looking for something that comes from the heart.

Your contribution could simply be a description of a place in Europe that means something to you. Or a description of a European.

I don't want to be prescriptive, but anecdote might well be a part of it and a theme might emerge, whether personal or cultural or both.

There's a passage in Saul Bellow's *The Dean's December* that's stayed with me. Hearing a dog barking forlornly in the night, the narrator intuits that it is protesting against the narrowness of its existence, saying: 'For God's sake, open the universe a little more!' The overall theme of this book, the overall question is: how has Europe made life in the UK wider, richer, deeper, happier or more vivid and pleasurable? Has it brought us new ideas on what it means to be human, to be alive or to be in love?

The responses to this email were moving. Many cared deeply enough to write beautiful, telling pieces. There are contributors who are famous partly because they have won the Booker, the Costa or other literary prizes, there are those who have written international bestsellers, or who have changed the face of global popular culture because they have reinvented comic books, for example, or sold 100 million albums or made movies or TV series viewed and well-loved not only in Britain but all over the world. Others are not yet household names but write with equal depth of insight and feeling.

There is some extraordinary writing in this book. It features some deeply personal stories, including anecdotes from child-hood and tragic stories from family history as well as from European history. A sense of place often sets in. There are exquisite, twisting sentences that take a thought for a walk. There is prose that fizzes on the page. There are cries of pain and regret. Some pieces are quietly devastating.

There are also expressions of a deep-seated and irrepressible impulse in our culture – the one that says when two or three Brits are gathered together at least one of you must take the piss. There are hilarious pieces here too.

Conceived as a love letter to Europe, this book throws a side-light on what's loveable about Britain – that richness and diversity again. Put all these people together in front of a camera and you'd have something like the cover of *Sgt Pepper*. The spirit of it also reminds me of the wonderful Blake-imbued opening ceremony of the London 2012 Olympic Games, shortly before the mood of public life turned sour.

The book begins with a sort of overture. Simply called 'A love letter to Europe', this section is a selection of pieces introducing both the book's themes and its variety of styles.

What follows is a series of nine sections which together form a sort of narrative of the different stages of love as it might go between individuals. So the first stage is called 'Love at first sight'. The idea of falling in love at first sight entered the stream of European consciousness and writing with the troubadours and Dante. When Shakespeare used the phrase in *As You Like It* ('Whoever loved that loved not at first sight') he was quoting from Marlowe's 'Hero and Leander'. The next section is called 'Let me count the ways', from the poem by Elisabeth Barrett Browning, famous eloping lover and Florence resident. The third section is called 'Come live with me': (Marlowe again, 'Come live with me and be my love', the first line of his poem 'The Passionate Shepherd to His Love'). The fourth section is called

'Opening the universe a little more' – from the passage in Saul Bellow's *The Dean's December* mentioned above. Here contributors explore how Europe has immeasurably increased our emotional, intellectual and cultural bandwidth. The pieces in the fifth section 'My North, my South, my East and West' make the point that we are so enmeshed in Europe that we *are* European. The idea that we live under a 'European sky' recurs in Auden, including in 'A Summer Night', his love poem to Geoffrey Hoyland, while 'My North, my South . . .' is from 'Funeral Blues'. The sixth section is called 'If music be the food of love', (from the opening of *Twelfth Night*) and it reprises some of the themes of the previous two sections with a musical twist.

There is a darkening of tone and mood in the seventh section, which addresses the pain of separation. The phrase '*Angoisse des gares*' sounds as if it comes from a Baudelaire or Verlaine, but I've been unable to trace it back further than where I first read it, in *The Unquiet Grave* by Cyril Connolly using the pen name Palinurus. We had asked writers not to be political – except of course in the sense that everything is political – but noticed that they increasingly tended to disregard this, perhaps partly because during the course of a month the country became more deeply divided and the national mood more anxious. The phrase that starts the eighth section, 'Reckless with others' hearts' has been attributed to both Kurt Vonnegut and Jimi Hendrix and turns up in a lyric by Baz Luhrmann, but the earliest recorded usage is by Mary Schmich, a columnist with the *Chicago Tribune*.

Some contributors make the point that where politics divides, culture can get to work and bring us back together. The ninth section is full of hope, and the title 'The love you take' comes, of course, from the last song of *Abbey Road* by the Beatles.

'All shall be well, and all shall be well and all manner of things shall be well.' So said the British medieval mystic Mother Julian of Norwich. Does anyone feel certain of that? Probably not, but reading this book and being reminded of British people's sensitivity, intelligence, good humour and longing for love, may help you feel a little more hopeful.

MB
9th September 2019

A LOVE LETTER TO EUROPE

IT BEGAN ON A FIELD IN NORMANDY

Penelope Lively

We are seventeen, sitting in a field somewhere in Normandy in 1950. I am English, Catherine is French. We are giggling, because we have got hold of some nail polish and are painting our nails, which Catherine's mother dislikes. And we talk non-stop. We talk in French. This is my gap year – some of us had them, even back then – and I am spending it as guest of Catherine's family, in Paris, and here at their summer bolthole in Normandy. Over the last months I have, by some osmotic process, become able to speak French. Not learned, just absorbed, by being in France, surrounded by the people, the language, and all that that implies.

And I am eternally grateful for that; it has given me some sort of enlargement of the mind – I wish I had more languages. I have hardly spoken French since – only on occasion when the French edition of a novel of mine came out and my French editor would summon me to do press interviews: 'Your French is quite good enough.' And it just about was, back in the eighties. It isn't now; I would find it hard to carry on a conversation in French. But the strange thing is that it is all there still, in the head, as a kind of sediment. Sometimes the French for some English word, or expression, will pop up, and I am surprised that I know it – I have not needed it for over sixty years.

After that gap year, I went to university to read history. The history curriculum in those days was sternly Eurocentric – forget America, Asia, elsewhere. So I emerged with some basic familiarity with European history, most of which seemed to be about wars. One kind of reality, I suppose – historical reality. But over the next decades came the discovery of a different kind of reality, for the islanders that we British are – the fascination of a landmass in which one country adjoins another, and all are significantly different. Their languages are different, they eat differently, their customs are different, their people look different, behave differently, think differently. This has made travel in Europe a matter of constant revelation: you are in Sweden, and think suddenly of a time when you were in Greece, a world apart, it seems, but still Europe, this amazing conglomeration of nations that is also a geographical unity. For me, because of that seminal long-ago year, there is always a sense of familiarity when I am back in France. More than that, the Channel is not a division; it is the route over to the continent with which our own history is inextricably enmeshed – centuries of mutual involvement. Our past is European; we are European.

FRED

Sandi Toksvig

I like peace and quiet. I work in showbusiness and most days are a bombardment of bright lights, chatter and loud noise often signifying nothing. I live my life in Britain, which I love, but when I have time to myself I escape to the place where I was born – Denmark. Just north of Copenhagen there is a glorious beach from which you can look out across the narrow Øresund strait that separates Denmark from Sweden. The waters are often wild, and the beach is usually windy, and I love to walk along hearing the unchanged sounds of my childhood. It is a place of immense calm. This stretch of sandy shore lies moments from where I came into the world and from where my grandparents had their home. It is a place that lies at the very heart of my Danish ancestry and I think these things matter. It is sometimes surprising how much we reflect the past in our present lives.

My grandfather died the week I was born and my grandmother when I was only about four, so I can't say I knew them. Nevertheless, something strong is inherited from them for I have pursued much the same line of work as they did. Indeed, it is as though I went into the family business. Farfar (Danish for Father-Father) was a writer and a painter while Farmor (Father-Mother) was an actress. I write and I dissemble so there must be something in the blood.

5

In 1939, when the Second World War broke out, my grandparents were living in Copenhagen, writing and acting. Although Germany and Denmark share a border, at first the conflict stayed south. Then, on 9 April 1940 the Germans moved north and invaded Denmark. Life for the Danes changed forever. At first the Germans wanted Denmark to appear cooperative, a model protectorate, so the repressions and rules were lightly applied, but they existed nonetheless. Many did not take kindly to any of it. Farmor became an active member of the resistance and even my father, aged just eleven, became a messenger for the underground movement.

In the first year or so of occupation what the Germans called the 'Jewish Problem' was not raised with the Danes. In fact, when the Great Synagogue in Copenhagen was subjected to arson, the perpetrators were dealt with severely by the Danish authorities. Denmark did not have a large Jewish population. There were just under 8,000 members of the faith living across the country. As far as I am aware my grandparents didn't know any Jews personally but, in the autumn of 1943, word was leaked that the Jews of Denmark were to be deported to concentration camps. Without further thought my family, along with many others, went into action. On 29 September the Danish Jews were warned by the Chief Rabbi of Denmark to go into hiding immediately.

Farfar built a false wall in the apartment and painted it to look like the end of their sitting room. Behind this theatrical piece of set he and Farmor concealed Jewish families on the run. My father, still a little boy, went door to door, removing Jewish names from doorbells and replacing them with ordinary Danish ones. One day my grandparents got word that the German authorities were coming to raid the apartment. Farmor took a knife and cut her legs with it before applying theatrical makeup to the wounds. When the men arrived, she was lying on a sofa giving her finest acting performance of ill health. The terrible running sores on her legs persuaded the invaders they did not want to stay. The apartment was not searched, and the hidden family not found.

Sweden was neutral in the war and on 2 October that year the Swedish government announced its willingness to take all Danish Jews. This land of freedom lay just ten miles or so across open water. Fishermen up and down the coast began to gather with any boat they could find. Some were large, some just kayaks. Along isolated stretches of the coast the great escape to Sweden began. Across the Øresund the exodus of the Jews began. Not every Dane behaved well and not every German behaved badly. Life is not that clear-cut but in the end over 99 per cent of the Danish Jews escaped the Holocaust. It was the finest example of cooperation in the face of injustice. My family had no reason to risk their lives for strangers but when I asked my father why they had done it he simply shrugged and said, 'It was the right thing to do.'

I think of this when I walk on that beach and look out to the stretch of sea that was once the site of that astonishing rescue. I hope I would have the same courage to do the right thing. I tell the story of what happened because history matters. Since the end of the Second World War and the wonderful decision by European countries to work together, we have had peace. Almost 75 years of it. I love peace and quiet. I love Europe.

A LARGER LIFE

Alan Hollinghurst

It's hard now to remember the boat-train and even the ferry itself, beyond the unstoppable moment when it cast off, the catch of the breath as the quay stepped sideways and everything re-aligned. What will never be forgotten is the sense of impatience for the other side, for Calais, Amiens, Paris. To learn how to get from the Gare du Nord to the Gare de Lyon, to find a room and order a beer and a *croque monsieur*, was to take command of a larger life, something we'd been raised and readied for and where we felt at once we belonged. Mile after mile, night after day, the journey went on: Marseille, Ventimiglia, Turin, Milan, possibilities turning to practical certainties, even Venice itself. This was something much larger and deeper than a holiday. We knew we belonged in Europe as our own country belonged there; all my adult life has been spent as a citizen of Europe as well as of Britain, each thing felt keenly to be both a privilege and a right. The mood, the madness, of our time is to destroy concord, cooperation, and as an inevitable result to destroy ourselves. If it's already too late to halt the destruction, it is also too late to efface the knowledge that we share in our millions, that we are Europeans.

WRITING HOME

J.K. Rowling

The letter was written on thin, pale blue paper. The handwriting was neat and rounded. My brand-new German pen friend, Hanna, introduced herself in excellent English. Our schools had decided that Hanna and I would be a good fit as pen pals because we were both, not to put too fine a point on it, swots. In a matter of months, I'd be going to stay with her Stuttgart-based family for a week, and shortly after that, she'd come and stay on the Welsh border, with me. I was thirteen. The whole thing was thrilling.

Her house was warm, spotless and deliciously different. I remember ornamental candles, and rugs on a tiled floor, the furniture sleek and well-designed, and a shining upright piano in the corner, which Hanna, of course, played very well. On arrival, Hanna's mother asked me what I wanted for breakfast, and when I didn't immediately answer, she began listing all the foodstuffs she had available. Around about item six or seven, I recognised the German for cake, so I said, 'Cake, please.'

Hanna's mother was a magnificent cook. I particularly remember the clear soup with dumplings and the sausage with lentils, and every morning of my visit, presumably because she thought that's what I was used to, she gave me cake for breakfast. It was glorious.

I kept in touch with Hanna for years, and when I was fifteen, the family invited me, with incredible generosity, to accompany them on a month-long trip to Italy. So, it was with Hanna and her family that I first saw the Mediterranean and first tasted shellfish.

I came home from Italy thirsty for more European adventures. I got myself a French pen pal called Adele, with whom in due course I went to stay in Brittany. There I watched her mother make crêpes, the region's speciality, on the *bilig*, a large, circular griddle: they were the most delicious things I'd ever eaten, even including the Italian lobster. When out of sight of adults, I took advantage of the cheapness of French cigarettes and practiced my nascent smoking habit, trying really hard to like *Gitanes*, and almost succeeding.

When I turned sixteen, my best friend and I cooked up the idea of going backpacking in Austria for a couple of weeks. Looking back, I do slightly wonder what our parents were thinking, letting us go: two schoolgirls with a smattering of German heading off on a coach with no fixed plans and no accommodation booked. We emerged from the experience unscathed: we successfully read the foreign train timetables, always managed to find accommodation, swam in ice-cold mountain lakes under brilliant sunlight and travelled from town to town as the fancy took us.

As I grew older, my determination to cross the Channel, even if alone or with insufficient funds, grew. If you had an Interrail ticket, surely one of the best inventions of all time, you could simply catch another train if you couldn't find a room, or else doze in the station until the next one arrived. I took off alone at nineteen to wander around France, a jaunt that ended abruptly with the theft of my wallet.

However, I was soon back again, because I spent a year in Paris as part of my French degree. My mother, a quiet Francophile with a half-French father, was delighted to visit me there; my father, possibly less so, given my perennially unsuccessful pleas to waiters to understand that '*bien cuit*' in his case meant *there must be no pink at all in the middle of the steak.*

I was twenty-five when my mother died, at which point I stopped pretending I wanted any kind of office job. Now I did what came most naturally: grabbed the dog-eared manuscript of the children's book I'd been writing for a few months and took off across the Channel again. Disorientated with grief, I'd chosen one of the three teaching jobs offered to me almost at random. It was in Portugal, a country I didn't know, and where I couldn't speak a word of the language.

Teaching English abroad is a perfectly respectable profession, but nobody who's done it can deny that it attracts its fair share of misfits and runaways. I was both. Nevertheless, I fell in love with Oporto and I love it still. I was enchanted by *fado*, the melancholy folk music that reflects the Portuguese themselves, who in my experience have a quietness and gentleness unique among Latin peoples I'd encountered so far. The city's spectacular bridges, its vertiginous riverbanks, steep with ancient buildings, the old port houses, the wide squares: I was entranced by them all.

We all have shining memories of our youth, made poignant because they're freighted with knowledge of what happened later to companions, and what lay ahead for ourselves. Back then we were allowed to roam freely across Europe in a way that shaped and enriched us, while benefitting from the longest uninterrupted spell of peace this continent has ever known. Lifelong friendships, love affairs and marriages could never have happened. Several children of my acquaintance, including my own eldest daughter, wouldn't have been born without the frictionless travel the EU gave us.

At the time of writing, it's uncertain whether the next generation will enjoy the freedoms we had. Those of us who know exactly how deep a loss that is, are experiencing a vicarious sense of bereavement, on top of our own dismay at the threatened rupture of old ties.

I think again of my teenage pen friend Hanna, as I reach for a quotation by Voltaire. She rarely let me get away with anything, so she'd probably have accused me of choosing a French philosopher in a spirit of pure provocation.

Well, Hanna was right about many things, but on this she'd be wrong. The truth is that I'm thinking of her now because she was my first friend from continental Europe, and because the words of Voltaire that hold so much meaning for me now are these: '*L'amitié est la patrie.*' 'Where there is friendship, there is our homeland.' And Hanna, I really don't want to lose my homeland.

MY STUDIO IN THE SOUTH OF FRANCE

Tracey Emin

I love my little studio in France – it's surrounded by nature, resting in a tiny valley.

In the winter there is a babbling brook that runs alongside the building. It flows into the vanishing lake that's only there from November to March. When I'm tucked inside working away, I feel safe nestled between the rolling hills and crimson skies. The light is magical. It's only recently that I have really understood why the Impressionists were so infatuated with light. The alchemy of time – the memory of light – impossible to capture. I don't try, I just watch it come and go.

Recently, looking through the window of my studio, I saw something move in the distance. It was a large fawn-coloured deer. We stared at each other; it made me feel like I was really part of nature. I make some of my best work in this tiny studio – because I feel free. There's enough room for me to work on nine canvases at once. Sometimes I work until two or three in the morning, painting like a banshee, like a mad conductor in a storm, running from one canvas to another until I'm exhausted and burnt out. Then, in the darkness, I go up to the house sometimes with confidence, unafraid, skipping around the olive trees under the moon. Day will soon break, and all is so beautiful in my creative world.

TWIN TOWNS

Sam Jordison

One of my strongest recollections from that vague, awkward period between childhood and puberty is of the day the deputation from Aalborg visited my hometown, Lancaster.

To understand why this visitation was so memorable, you have to trudge in my black and clumpy school shoes for a while. Every day after lessons ended, my friends and I were cast adrift for an hour or more among the dismal shops of early nineties Lancaster, while we waited for the buses that would finally take us home. We walked aimlessly through useless empty time. We knew every single record that Our Price stocked. Waterstones hadn't arrived yet. We weren't allowed in the pubs. We weren't welcome in the tea shops. (Yes, tea shops. There weren't any cafes back then.) We were desperate for distraction.

So we were as grateful as we were surprised when a half-dozen or so smiling and pleasingly handsome Danish people one day took over a shop near the town hall to put on a display about their home. Did we want to know about 'the city of smoking chimneys' and its early twentieth-century cement factories? Well, sure, since they were asking and since they were also offering to feed us cheese and herrings.

Aalborg, I learned that day, was Lancaster's twin town. It was a medium-sized Danish city with a rich medieval history that had more recently suffered industrial decline. It had a cool (verging on cold) climate and plenty of annual rainfall. I had to admit that all that did sound a bit like Lancaster. But we were still sceptical about the twin-town concept, even as we noshed happily on the fish products and looked appreciatively at the clean lines of the pine furniture our new friends had installed in the shop. But would many citizens of a twin town really want to come over to our rainy bit of northern England to share in our boredom?

The answer to that question did turn out to be a cautious 'yes'. It turned out that the burghers of Lancaster had quite an enthusiasm for twinning. They had somehow managed to trick their fellow dignitaries in Perpignan in the sunny south of France to hook up with them, too. And so, a few years after that astonishing Danish visitation, my school arranged an exchange with our Mediterranean counterparts and a coachload of French teenagers duly arrived on our doorstep.

To our great surprise, our *amis* seemed to like Lancaster. My exchange partner, the not particularly French-sounding Sven, was absolutely fascinated by the pubs I was too young to get into. He was also impressed by the tiny patina of cool that had rubbed off on the town thanks to its relative proximity to Madchester. The Stone Roses – or any other worthwhile band – had never actually visited our one tiny music venue, but Sven didn't need to know that. Nor did he seem to care. It was enough to be in the North of England. He and his compatriots even seemed impressed by the shops that we found so tedious and by the local architecture, which we had long since stopped noticing.

I felt guilty, all the same. It rained the whole time they were with us – and I just knew we were going to have a better time when we did the return leg later on that summer.

I was right. Whereas my school had arranged visits to a broken-down amusement park in the failing resort of Morecambe and to a nuclear power station in Heysham, in France they took us to the beach, to water parks and to an astonishing Salvador Dali museum. What's more, everything we did was bathed in glorious sunshine. But the best thing about my part of the exchange turned out to be Sven's dad, Robert Gaubert.

Pretty much the first thing that Monsieur Gaubert explained to me when I arrived at his house was that he was a psychologist and a sexologist.

A sexologist.

This idea was terrifying. I knew that Monsieur Gaubert would instantly be able to tell that I was a Massive Virgin. He'd realise that I'd barely spoken to a girl, let alone held hands with one or engaged in any of the rest of that mysterious business.

But I had no reason to be afraid. Even in my teenage solipsism, I came to understand that he didn't care how fast or slow I was developing. And it was impossible to be intimidated by him for long. He was funny and silly and kind. He spoke to me, if not as an adult (my French wasn't good enough for that), at least as a friend. He asked my opinion about everything he could think of, he tirelessly tried to teach me local idioms, he laughed at my mistakes instead of finding them annoying, and he spent hours with Sven and me (not to mention his other two kids) every day keeping us entertained and amused.

La famille Gaubert took me scuba diving in the Mediterranean. They took me walking in the Pyrenees and bathing in hot springs. They showed me Roman ruins. They took me to meet relatives in Spain to slurp Gazpacho. They took me to fireworks for the 14 July. They took me – bizarrely – to a fashion show where Monsieur

Gaubert gleefully explained that half of the models were clients of his. What on earth did a sexologist actually do?

Looking back now I can understand how proud Monsieur Gaubert must have been of his home and how keen he was to show it to me. I also now realise that this kind man had taken on the wider project of helping to bring me into the world.

I was quite an odd teenager. As well as worrying about girls and cultivating boredom, I most liked listening to The Cure, reading Victorian novels and learning Latin verb formations. All fine things – but perhaps not ideal for building a fully socialised adult. Monsieur Gaubert understood this and became determined that I should start to relish more simple pleasures. That I should have fun. He set about bringing me out of my shell – and also, in his wisdom and benevolence, he supplied me with the perfect metaphor for this process. He took me to a snail-eating festival.

This event – which had the significant bonus of being the most French thing I could imagine – took place in parkland, on long plastic tables, in the gentle early evening sun. Monsieur Gaubert kept us in blissful ignorance about the financial arrangements, but the basic deal seemed to be that after you got a ticket and sat down, you were given limitless supplies of good crispy French bread, alongside as many escargots cooked in a delicious garlic sauce as you could eat. Also: red wine. This latter was a crucial part of Monsieur Gaubert's design. He had decided that it was time I got drunk. Not English drunk. Not roaring, fighting or puking. Just gently glowing and merry. He encouraged me to imbibe just enough to set me talking volubly in suddenly improved French and giggling at everything everyone else said.

Everyone else must have been enjoying the wine too, because at some hazy point in the evening, they all started throwing snail shells at each other amidst uproarious laughter, *ooh-là-làs*, *putains* and other French expressions of surprise and glee. I recall the singular satisfaction of a well-flicked shell hitting its target. I remember Monsieur Gaubert laughing and patting me on the back and encouraging me to target anyone and everyone. Also, before the night blurs into forgetfulness, I have a glorious final image of myself standing on a plastic chair in a hail of snail shells, lobbing bread and friendly insults at a nearby Frenchman. What greater happiness could there be?

Well, I was on the way to finding out. I'll be forever grateful to Monsieur Gaubert for pointing me towards it. He was a lovely man. And Perpignan has remained one of my favourite places. I visit as often as I can. Partly because the south-west of France is so beautiful, partly because it has such warm associations, and partly because I feel such kinship with the place. It reminds me of Lancaster. I love it for that. It's funny how things work out.

AU REVOIR

Sebastian Faulks

From where we live in the south of England, it's a bit of a hike to the Welsh marches or the Scottish borders. But it's only a short drive down to Folkestone and then . . .

France. Suddenly you are through the looking-glass, among a people who do not share a single one of our views about ourselves, *them*selves, history, culture, patriotism, food, ethics, love or life itself. It's a wonderland and a lifetime study, just twenty miles away – closer than Birmingham. Push east through Alsace-Lorraine, however, and you'll find a people who are much more like us, almost weirdly so, which is one of the reasons why Berlin, with its Holocaust memorials and Stasi dungeons, is so unsettling – and another reason why the foreignness of Boulogne is so remarkable.

I first experienced continental Europe in Portugal, in a white-washed breeze-block bungalow with no electricity. I was eleven and was told to pump water from the well. Everything seemed intense: the midday heat, the orange-fleshed melons with their bark-like skins, the exploding grapes and peaches, the kerosene lamps by whose light we ate dinner, the phosphorescence that trailed from your hand in a midnight swim. There was a five-mile beach with no one on it, until Sunday, when the villagers came down in black clothes to give their pigs a sand bath. The unmade street is under concrete or asphalt now, I imagine, and the wine shop with *vinho tinto* at five escudos a flagon is probably a yoga studio. But it did exist, once.

Then there was Deauville and the *Beau Séjour* boarding house, on which Jacques Tati had surely based Monsieur Hulot's holiday hotel. The ride in a hydraulic Citroen DS taxi, the sandy tennis court, a fizzy drink named 'Pschitt!', the little foot-baths in the rooms called 'bidets', the pet dogs fed at table in the dining room and the dishes that issued from the swing doors of the kitchen in a bewitching stream . . . The public lavatories with two footholds and nothing to cling on to and the hilarious attempts at pop music on the radio.

Then Spain, the Costa Brava, and the night club that played '*Je t'aime, moi non plus*' while we drank sangria by the bucket. The smoky paella at lunch time, the stickiness of prawn and chicken that was in breach of some sacred Catalonian recipe but sated teenage appetites sharpened by hours of swimming and gazing at girls too old for us.

Two years later, aged eighteen, there was hitchhiking across the entire continent from La Rochelle to Istanbul, when finally Europe became culture as well as food, as we reeled in amazement in the galleries of Florence (a little anxious that our school-room Pre-Raphaelite posters didn't quite match up to . . . well, Raphael), the Caravaggio churches of Rome, the Parthenon and the Greek islands where we slept on the sand, lived on sixpence a day (including retsina) and there was almost no one there, in Samos, in Corfu, even Mykonos, except for a few like-minded escapists. We talked to American college students, who were incredulous, literally open-mouthed in some cases, at the glory that was Greece. We felt . . . proud. It was something, wasn't it?

Our elder son lives and works in Spain, our o.
ied in Aix and Verona and our youngest had expect.
course, to work in Europe too. It's no more than a New .
hoping for a spell in Michigan. And perhaps it may happe.
after a fashion, with more paperwork and queues and after we
have overcome the self-inflicted economic crash. I have met
only five people who voted to leave. None are bigots or 'racists';
each had sane or sophisticated reasons. Nor do I blame the
millions who apparently voted just to be heard, to protest at
being overlooked. Why shouldn't they protest? But I do blame
Remain's pathetic campaign and the lies of the Leavers. The
people who will suffer most are those who always do, the ones
least able to afford it; I don't imagine Mr Dyson or Mr Rees-
Mogg will have much trouble moving their fortunes round
offshore.

There is a large difference between Europe the place and
'Europe', the EU. And before we get too dewy-eyed about old
Europe, let's remind ourselves that the only thing the continent
led the world in during the twentieth century was genocide:
Stefan Zweig, scion of old Austria, killed himself in despair at
what Europe had become, in exile in Brazil in 1942. The EU itself
is smug, secretive and unlovable; de Gaulle's betrayal of his
wartime saviours when we first tried to join was a disgrace. But
the EU is something, a stumbling step, a source at least of funds
for science, farming and research, a centripetal force in a fissile,
war-prone continent. And to be better than it is, to be worthy of
representing the best of Europe, it needed the country of
Shakespeare and Newton to be a part of it.

Europe itself is like the Addams or the Royal Tenenbaum
families. There are no forgettable sisters or shy brothers.

Austria-Hungary, the Paris Commune, Garibaldi and Leonardo, Bach and Goering, Pasteur, Waterloo, the Somme and Don Quixote, Mary Stuart, Ibsen, Einstein and Voltaire, Joan of Arc, Erasmus, Kepler, Buchenwald, Sibelius, Van Gogh, Greta Garbo, Proust, Praxiteles and Wordsworth . . . the EU has not yet risen to the challenge of reflecting that noise, that concentration of human vitality, good and evil, but maybe no institution really could. Now it will have to soldier on without one of its main players, an orchestra in which a section has been silenced.

But the band plays on. *Auf wiedersehen* – and keep my seat. *Grazie per tutto. À la prochaine . . .*

NIKI LAUDA AT THE HOTEL IMPERIAL

Patrick Lenox

The man sitting to my left, at a corner table of the breakfast room at the Hotel Imperial on the Kärntner Ring in Vienna, was badly burnt, but not beyond recognition. In fact, the opposite was true. His scars were unmistakably those of the great racing driver Niki Lauda. He ate quietly on his own, a solitary figure taking in the news with his copy of the *Wiener Zeitung* and sipping one of the city's famous coffees, a *Brauner Verlängerter*. It was the third time I had seen him in as many weeks, always at the same table and always alone, never fussed over by the staff and never disturbed by fellow breakfasters in the know. Their quiet conversations ebbed and flowed around the room, impossible to catch with any certainty, muffled and muted by the heavy curtains and velvet furnishings in the former home of the Prince of Württemberg.

I was new to Vienna at the time, only a month or two into my posting and still tipsy on the cocktail of sights and sounds that the city poured over my senses. I was still taking in the contradictions of the old capital of the Austro-Hungarian Empire – a modern city where you can nevertheless hear your own footfall and smell the manure on the cobbled streets around the Stephansdom, where the clinking horse-drawn carriages, bell-ringing trams and silent gliding metros join together in a medley of ancient, old and new.

By the time I took up my post there, Vienna had given up its imperial ambitions, knocked sideways by two world wars, stranded and somewhat exposed – the most easterly Western capital in Europe, further east and closer to Russia even than Prague. Somehow it had preserved much of its Habsburg charm, despite the war damage and the threat from the East, as an elegant crossroads absorbing peoples and influences from the edges of Europe and beyond.

I had been sent to the embassy and it was my job to make sense of some of these contradictions, to turn them to advantage and build discreet alliances with those of its inhabitants or visitors who might be helpful if approached in the right way. The brief was clear – to use subtlety and guile to gather knowledge on our main adversaries, using the resources and relationships available in Europe's oldest and most revered centre of espionage.

It took me a while to work it out, to understand that the city existed to welcome foreigners and let them play their games. Vienna provided the perfect backdrop to the non-stop chess marathon being played by the world powers; their officials, diplomats and spies jockeying for advantage as they occupied their favourite meeting places in the city's cellared restaurants, grand old coffee houses and palatial hotels. And this was a game that went on without causing a ripple or a stir. Vienna was too polite to intervene or object, had too much to gain by turning a blind eye, too much to lose by stepping in the way.

Lauda seemed to me to personify what the city was all about – his scars were worn with neither shame nor pride and they had done nothing to diminish his stature. His quiet greatness, like that of Vienna's finest buildings and statues, was acknowledged silently and without show.

In the city, the scars of war are still visible too; they can be seen but, with the odd exception, easily pass unnoticed. Apart from the few, indestructible, concrete flak towers that rise to the roof level of the surrounding apartments at the edge of Vienna's central district, memorials to last century's greatest atrocities are hard to find. Vienna razed and rebuilt its Gestapo headquarters as an apartment block with a print shop and dermatologist on the ground floor, at the edge of the Danube in the Innere Stadt; its Jewish memorial is equally discreet and few visitors to the Albertina Museum would ever know that the small triangle of park beside it is a permanent shrine to the 200 dead, buried alive in the cellars below the grass by a direct hit on the Philipphof by Allied bombers, in 1945. Vienna does not advertise its scars but hasn't hidden them either. They are available for the curious to discover, for those who really want to find out – half-known secrets in the city of the *Third Man*.

And what of Vienna's glories? The imperial palaces, state buildings, opulent coffee houses, ballrooms and theatres? They continue to thrive, not to accommodate a long-since forgotten European aristocracy but to sustain the hordes of paying visitors from around the world, all seeking some connection with a greater, more beautiful past. The Riesenrad still turns in the Prater, spawning countless photo opportunities in Orson Welles poses, while diners at the Schweizerhaus still demolish mountains of pork knuckle and sauerkraut, washed down with gurgling rivers of beer. Like the Prater theme park, there is something for everyone in this city, a little old-fashioned but a lot of fun, if you know where to look and who to ask.

A city of waltzes and wurlitzers, *Kaffee und Küchen*, tunnels and traps: we knew it as the playground of spies. Vienna had to make itself relevant in the new world order after the end of the war and spying was the way. Divided between the great powers, its citizens understood the value of quiet negotiation and compromise as they crossed from sector to sector, finding ways to make themselves useful and win favour with their occupiers. A message delivered clandestinely here, a package dropped off there, the keys to an apartment pressed into the hands of a furtive official at a checkpoint late at night. The business of espionage and intrigue has sustained the city's economy as surely as the tourists queuing at the entrance to Schönbrunn and the Belvedere. Hundreds of diplomats – some genuine, many not – now tread the corridors of the UN agencies dealing with nuclear issues and security cooperation in Europe; that both were established in Vienna comes as no surprise.

Austria was late to embrace Europe, joining, with Sweden and Finland, in 1995. The move did nothing to change the politics, or power, that swings from left to right and back again with the reliability of an old pendulum, balancing red with black and settling in the middle with an accommodation of key positions handed out to both sides to maintain the equilibrium. There will be no more revolutions here, nor any nostalgic attempts to return to a more powerful past, no moves to take back some notion of national sovereignty. Untroubled by Brussels, the smokers will still smoke in the restaurants and bars (in their own separate areas, of course), the Riesenrad will keep on turning, the spies will keep on spying; alliances will keep forming. And the scars of the city will remain, as testament both to its past and to its enduring resilience in a modern, more confusing world. Niki Lauda is no more, but his mark is indelible, imprinted on him by the city of his birth, and returned with interest: burnt but unbroken, quietly glittering, unyielding through the fire.

Sleep well, Niki. Goodnight, Vienna.

SETTING OUR FACES TO THE SUN

Heather Cooper

My father was captured during the battle of Crete and spent the rest of the war in various prisoner-of-war camps in Poland and Germany, the last being Colditz. One might have expected this experience to have put him off mainland Europe as a whole and perhaps Germany in particular.

Au contraire, as he would never have said. From the time I was two (in 1958), my family hitched up a Bluebird caravan to the elderly shooting brake or, later, fixed the Tent-O-Matic on to the car roof, and drove every summer from northern Lancashire to the Channel ports, and on to France, Germany, Austria, Italy.

Castles of dream-like beauty. Alpine meadows where the toffee-brown cattle wore bells that chimed as they wandered through flowers. Ancient towns, a jumble of russet roofs and narrow winding streets clinging to steep hillsides. Cool misty campsite mornings with the sun rising over a blue river. Once, we travelled to Greece – by train – and stayed in a house yards from the dazzling sea, where we ate every meal in the shade of olive trees and vines.

And oh, the food! Post-war austerity still lingered in Britain. On our travels we ate yoghurt (in little waxed paper pots), black cherry jam (from tins rather than jars), garlicky sausages, croissants, pumpernickel bread, tiny green grapes that tasted of honey. Huge tomatoes stuffed with rice, lamb grilled and blackened and fragrant with oregano. Buckwheat pancakes full of smoked ham and melted cheese. We never ate in fancy restaurants, just bought food in ordinary shops or stopped at roadside taverns.

Did my father want to take his family to these foreign places just for the food, or the scenery? There must have been some appalling memories for him there. He'd been hungry, ill; he saw friends die. But we went back, year after year, and during the winter months he listened to Linguaphone records to keep up his spoken German and Greek, so that he could greet, talk, laugh with, the people we met abroad.

The war seemed so remote when I was a child. Now I realise it was only a few short years before those rackety holidays that Europe had been torn apart. Dad set his face to the sun, however, and so did we all, and the shadow of war fell behind, and we came back every year full of memories, full of warmth and amazement, full of croissants and black cherry jam, full of happiness.

LOVE AND SQUALOR

Simon Evans

My first ineradicable memory of Europe centres on Marseilles. I am of course just guessing, but my suspicion is that many of my fellow epistolary contributors will be pointing to an elevating exposure to high culture, or a sudden romance, or some architectural splendour unmatched on our miserable windswept pagan rock. But as we bid farewell to Europe this autumn, and banish its memory from our hearts, I think of my first taste of Her as being one of magnificent, unapologetic squalor.

An aristocratic nineteenth-century *ingénu*, upon arrival at Calais docks and preparing for the Grand Tour, is famously said to have enquired as to the nature of the predominant aroma, and was told by his worldly (paid) companion, 'That, my Lord, is the Continent.' The drains have vastly improved since then and, indeed, a similar odour is of course blamed in rest homes across southern England on precisely the reverse demographic. But it was certainly in evidence as my companion and I disembarked from the ferry on 5 July 1983.

This was my first unchaperoned visit and I was travelling with my best friend – which he remains to this day. Ross Cohen, my virtual twin, born the day before me, and a man whose life I now know was even more deeply intertwined with mine than I had then guessed. But this was to be our great bonding experience.

We spent eight weeks hitchhiking across Europe, all the way to Athens and back, on a capital sum that halved, like some travel budget paradox of Xeno's, roughly every week, yet never seemed to finally disappear. I honestly would not have wished for even an ounce more credit or more glamour, let alone the absurd detachment and insulation from reality afforded the Interrailer.

Within two days of leaving Calais we were holed up with Bill Tingle, a Cheshire haulage man, in Relais Bourgogne. Bill had given us a lift only to get a puncture, and now we were parked in a service station halfway down the *autoroute du soleil*, watching a man covered in suspicious pustules and sores, who it turned out was on the run from the French Foreign Legion, urinate on a truculent wheel nut that had refused to loosen under the application of WD40, vinegar and diet coke. As we feared, this final remedy worked, and we thus had to spend the rest of the journey to Marseilles with four of us in the front of the cab. It was at this point that I learned to smoke.

Marseilles was the baptism of fire that everyone should have when leaving safe home counties homes for the first time. The Vieux Port was straight out of a Howard Hawks movie. The Arab Quarter is the standard by which I judge claims to 'vibrancy' in neighbourhoods to this day. And sleeping rough on the verges, beaches and railway terminals is, of all the things I have ever done, that of which my survival was statistically the most remarkable.

We went on to visit several of the world's great cities that summer, and also many of the world's great dumps, often docks and truck-stops and underpasses and other destinations symptomatic of choosing to travel by thumb. Piraeus, which serves Athens, was probably the pits. The undisposed dead dogs, the sheer quantity of greased metal, and the heavy fumes of diesel and heavier oils, all simmering in the effortless heat, combined to render a memorable vison of Hell. But Marseilles was my first love, and first love never ever dies.

A NEW EUROPEAN SONG

Mary Beard

This piece was written in 2016

A few days ago, I was one of a crowd of thousands in the ancient amphitheatre at Pompeii. It was the first time since AD 79 that an audience had gathered there to watch a show, not in this case a gladiatorial fight or a wild beast hunt, but a concert by David Gilmour, singer, guitarist and veteran of the rock band Pink Floyd. For me, it felt like a wonderful way both of stepping into Roman history and of enjoying a belated triumph over Roman brutality.

To be honest, we probably overestimate quite how bloody the games were at a backward little place like Pompeii. Gladiators were far too expensive a commodity to kill in large numbers in front of a local audience. But any traces of blood were now, for an evening at least, spectacularly obliterated by the fun, the fireworks and the very loud music.

It wasn't actually the first time that Gilmour had appeared in this amphitheatre. In 1971, when Edward Heath was busy negotiating Britain's entry into the Common Market, he had played there with the rest of the band to make the famous movie *Pink Floyd: Live at Pompeii*. But then it had been empty of all but the musicians, the cameras and the crew.

Gilmour's repeat of that occasion, by sheer coincidence a couple of weeks after Britain had voted itself out of the EU, was

33

instead in front of a heaving crowd that seemed to encapsulate some of the intriguing cultural entanglements of the New Europe. There we were, a polyglot gathering of young and old from different European countries, all happily colonising one of the most striking ruins of an ancient European empire that had once colonised us.

We were both sharing a memorable celebration and bringing our different experiences to the party, and taking away different messages. When Gilmour belted out one of Floyd's classic lines, 'Hanging on in quiet desperation is the English way,' the middle-aged British fans, me included, smiled at that wry joke, which was, I suspect, lost on most of the Italian teenagers.

But given the timing, I couldn't help thinking about the New Europe that we British seemed to be about to lose, and about my own personal stake in that. My career as an academic can be measured against the history of the Common Market, the EEC and the EU.

I left school in 1972, and over those last forty-something years, what I do, the context in which I do it, and how I define myself and my job has changed dramatically, taking a decidedly European turn that is, without doubt, a turn for the better. What's most important here is the broader intellectual and cultural world of which British universities have become a part.

I'm not just talking cash, though it's true that the consequences on UK research of the withdrawal of EU funding may be devastating. A bigger revolution has been going on in a way that would have seemed inconceivable when I was doing my own degree. I now expect to find students from all over Europe in my classes. Some of my closest colleagues in my department in Cambridge come from Italy, Germany and Greece.

It's a two-way traffic as our staff and students have come simply to assume that the Continent, as we used to call it, as if it wasn't us, is as open to them as the UK is, open for conversation, for resources and for collaboration. This doesn't just add to the local colour. The mixture of cultures and languages, of educational backgrounds and different traditions of expertise has widened all our horizons. And it has changed how we think about our subject, our opportunities, and even about the very nature of education itself.

To put it another way, whereas back in the eighties, I would have introduced myself as a British academic, maybe even an English one, I now also think of myself and call myself European, and I mean *also*. You don't give up feeling British when you start to feel European. One of the worst legacies of Norman Tebbit, in his infamous 'cricket test', was saddling us with the notion that cultural allegiance and sporting patriotism was an either/or kind of phenomenon.

Who did British Indians support when it came to the test match, he asked: India or England? That told you all you needed to know about where these immigrants' loyalties lay. Of course, it didn't tell you anything of the kind. Cultural identity is much more nuanced, much more multiple, and it doesn't work like Tebbit tendentiously suggested.

To go back to the world of the amphitheatre for a moment, this is one of the things that the ancient Romans got right, insisting as they did that you could be both Roman and Spanish and British, and so on. A person could, in their words, have more than one heart. In fact, one of my favourite characters from the ancient world made exactly that point on his tombstone.

He was a rich man called Zoilos, who came from a small town in what is now Turkey, but had made his fortune hundreds of miles away in Rome itself. On his grand memorial back home, he had himself depicted twice, once in a Roman toga and once in his native costume. It's what we might call being culturally ambidextrous. I suppose that's rather what I feel in the New Europe when I tingle a bit to the strains of 'Ode to Joy' as I do to 'God Save the Queen'.

It's a complexity and an openness that is something to celebrate. But there's another less optimistic side to it, and that comes down to the question of who exactly the beneficiaries of what I'm calling this New European culture have been. It's all very well for intellectuals to enjoy the new linguistic Babel of their common rooms, or of the students at elite universities to take advantage of the new horizons that come with cultural European collaboration. Or even, let's face it, the relatively well-heeled Gilmour fans to take a plane to a concert in the ruins of Pompeii.

But none of that means very much to the unemployed of, say, Boston, Lincolnshire. In cultural terms, in England at least, and I think Scotland may have done better, the new European project tended to be the project of those already privileged. My hunch is that that's one big reason why the referendum went the way it did.

Hardly any voter thought they could make head nor tail of the economic predictions. The specious propaganda about sovereignty, migration and getting our country back became powerful because it spoke to those who weren't necessarily racist or xenophobic, but who didn't in any way feel European. It's asking a lot to ask people to remain in the EU when Europe has always been a foreign country.

Those of us who have been the beneficiaries of New Europe must face the uncomfortable fact that we are partly to blame for the vote going, on our terms, so badly wrong. Because we didn't stop, or we didn't stop long enough, to think of those who are on the other side of the cultural divide. We didn't work hard enough over the decades, not just over the months of the referendum campaign, to share the benefits of which we were so certain and so rightly proud.

The succession of governments, back to the seventies, has a lot to answer for too. When, in a couple of hundred years' time, historians come to reflect on why Britain decided to quit the EU, they will, I'm sure, look in astonishment at how little those governments did to help us all think Europe. Cultural identity may be multiple, it may be nuanced, but it still needs working on.

To me, it simply beggars belief that while the UK was entirely reformulating its relations with the rest of Europe, we were still happy that many, if not most, children in schools were fed a history curriculum that was built on British heroism against Europe, in which fighting Germans on the beaches and escaping from Colditz were repeatedly presented as our finest hour.

It even more beggars belief, as will no doubt be observed by those historians in the future, that over these last decades, we have let Modern European languages in schools dangerously decline. German, in particular, has been in freefall, with 2016 marking its lowest ever GCSE entry. Maybe that's not wholly surprising. GCSEs put enormous emphasis on making yourself understood in a foreign language, which is fair enough. But as every canny teenager knows, speaking English slow and loud in a Colonel Blimpish way is likely to be a far better way of getting directions to the train station than your faltering German. Couldn't we have sold those languages more as a way of entering another culture, of opening our cultural eyes, and of being European?

Some of the most eloquent Brexiteers have ready answers to the worries that I'm raising. They would point, for a start, to a variety of other cultural traditions outside the EU, and I would be the first to admit that students and colleagues from the Americas, Australia and the Far East have also contributed to the diversity of the world in which I now work.

But they would also say that you didn't necessarily need the EU to underpin the cultural collaboration I have been praising. Some upmarket Eurosceptics, as they never cease to remind us, are the biggest Europhiles of all. They have European wives, husbands and partners, and in some cases, European second homes. I don't know how that plays in Boston, Lincs.

They love everything about Europe, from Mozart to Real Madrid, except any form of political integration, which they insist is not relevant to the cultural project. That has more to do with the Channel Tunnel and cheap air fares than anything coming out of Brussels. I see what they mean, but I don't think they're right.

Of course, Brexit will not spell the instant end to Euro-collaboration. We won't all retreat to an unadulterated diet of Morris dancing any more than Switzerland, outside the EU, has remained a country of cuckoo clocks. Some of the intellectual exchanges will be too embedded to scrap. And anyway, the rich have always been able to spend their time soaking up the atmosphere at European universities.

But for the rest of us, collaboration means institutional support and resources. We still don't know, for example, what will happen to the Erasmus scheme, which has so far supported more than 200,000 British students to work in the EU and its neighbours. The Erasmus website understandably, but unhelpfully, currently asks those who are anxious to be patient about the scheme's future. Definitive answers on the programme's future, particularly in relation to UK students in universities, may take time, it says.

If you want to know, I'm pessimistic. I can't help thinking that what's left of my working life will see the intellectual boundaries we thought we'd broken down closing up again. And that is what I felt next to the pleasure of the occasion in the amphitheatre at Pompeii the other evening when I was listening to Gilmour rather attentively.

Straight after the words about hanging on in the English way, came the even more ominous line, 'The time is gone, the song is over.' Sitting where so many ancient Romans had sat before, I did start to wonder if the whole thing wasn't a bit of a requiem. The excitement of my own particular New European song perhaps really was over.

THE MOON HIDDEN BY A CLOUD

Andrew Miller

My mother decided – I don't quite know what the evidence was, how solid – that we were French Huguenots. She thought it better, perhaps, than just coming from Essex, which is where she was born. All her life (the life I can remember) she worked to learn French. She had teach-yourself books, she had tapes, she took an adult education course at a local college. Later, she joined an informal French class that met once a fortnight at the home of the teacher, a beautiful and saintly woman called Sue. It was a conversation class; no one was trying to pass an exam. They wanted to speak French on their holidays. They wanted to be the kind of people who spoke French, who knew it. Some of them had houses in France or hoped they would do one day. At the end of each class Sue set them homework. They had to read an article photocopied from a French magazine; they had to write a letter to an imaginary friend in France, or perhaps to an *agent immobilier*. As the day of the class approached, my mother would sit at the old desk in the hall and do the work. It was no hardship. She was happy to do it.

When my stepfather's father died he left some money that my stepfather used to buy a small place outside Annecy, a new-build chalet, or part of one, in foothills that looked up to the mountains. On one wall they put up a poster of Cezanne's painting of

Lake Annecy. Every summer and Easter they drove down, usually on the quieter roads, staying at little hotels in small towns. They shopped at the market in Annecy. They made friends with the neighbours. They dug a garden and planted it with alpine flowers. They spent hours reading novels on the terrace while the mountains shone madly in the distance.

They kept the house for ten or fifteen years, then sold it. I don't know if the reason was financial or they were just getting tired of the long drive down. But though the house was gone and so the motive for studying the language must have felt smaller, my mother continued to attend the classes. Was she making any progress? There was, we believed, a lot of French inside her head but not much of it came out. We suspected her of wanting to replicate the elegant and spirited way she spoke English, but by the time she had constructed her sentence, had conjugated the verbs and found some unexpected adjective, the conversation had moved on.

After her first stroke at the age of sixty-nine she was still able to get to class if my stepfather drove her. After the second stroke she was too broken down, too demoralised, too ashamed of herself to go. Her teacher, who she had known now for many years, who was still beautiful and saintly, paid her visits, and sometimes (as I listened from the kitchen) there were short exchanges in French, always started by the teacher, as though she lit a match, sheltered the flame a moment, then passed it to my mother.

In the last months of her life most of my mother's out-of-bed hours were spent in a Parker Knoll recliner watching or not watching the television. On one of the padded white leatherette arms of the chair she wrote in biro (secretly, we never caught her at it), and though her writing had always tended towards scrawl, you could pick out, between the scribbling and the hieroglyphics, fragments of French – single words, a half-sentence. My stepfather, who had his own Parker Knoll on the other side of the room, told her off. At the same time he seemed to find it quite funny. They had both entered a place the rest of us were a little afraid of.

They died within a few months of each other, and because what I do involves paper and pens, I was given the old desk. In one of the deep drawers there were dozens of exercise books and journalists' notepads filled with work from the French classes. Years and years of it. There were also some of her textbooks – *French Verbs Simplified*, a Collins' bilingual dictionary, and a curious little book entitled *La Troisième Année de Grammaire*, intended, I think, for French schoolchildren; an edition from 1966, printed for (at?) the Librairie Armand Colin, 103 Boulevard Saint-Michel, Paris.

The notebooks, the homework, I threw away. When parents die there is so much to throw away; it becomes a kind of frenzy. But the little book of grammar, with its smooth, foxed pages, I kept. I'm not sure why. A piece of the past, a memento of an old ambition, an old passion. In its style – the numbered paragraphs, the graceful typeface – there is some sweet dream of clarity, or better still, of *clarté*, with its extra sense of shone light (moon/lamp). Throughout the book, faint pencil lines – marks that may or may not have been made by my mother – draw attention to what must have seemed, in passing, important or interesting. The orthography of numbers (paragraph 164); the proper use of *soi* (paragraph 197); an explanation of allegory (paragraph 648). Also, in a chapter introducing the past participle, the rules and pitfalls of, the following model sentence: *La lune est* cachée *par un nuage*.

This for what it taught of grammar or said of life.

IN THE PASSPORT QUEUE

Jeffrey Boakye

It's always at the airport. In that queue waiting to show your passport and be given entry into the country in question, with a sprint of thoughts rushing through the mind, competing fears about how and if you are going to be accepted. In that final step you always feel so other, so different, clinging to your British identity, leather-bound in red, hoping it will keep you buoyant in unfamiliar seas. That's the point when you feel most far from home; the wrong colour, in the wrong country, equipped with the wrong language and feeling the wrong cocktail of apprehensions.

But then, you get to the perspex booth, and something happens. There's a smile, or a chat, or a comment – some kind of exchange that reminds you that you belong, at least, to this moment. That it's not always aggression or suspicion. That sometimes, it's a welcome. You collect those moments, because they are valuable. You hope that they won't become rare.

OF SHOES – AND SHIPS – AND SEALING WAX
OF CABBAGES – AND KINGS

B. Catling

1981 Towards Europe by water; the old way.

The journey started by jetfoil from St Katherine Dock in the shadow of the Tower of London, where twenty-five years later I would make a glass monument for those executed at the whim of kings and queens. Gliding on the then empty Thames, skimming past unused defensive structures, some glorious in their heritage aspic, some rotting in the open sea, the craft eventually docked at Ostend. Enough time for seafood, pastis and *Boyards Caporal* cigarettes at a quayside restaurant before the train to Maastricht. The most Roman Catholic city in the Netherlands, Maastricht was powerful and proud of its wealth, carnival and crucifixions. I was a guest artist there at the Jan Van Eyck Academie.

Just across its south-west frontier sulked and brooded the city of Liège, trying not to remember its affluent past in the slough of its bankruptcy. On Sunday mornings I would be drawn to a part of the city that seethed. Rich in squalor and life, the Batte market was a Bruegel-esque throng of stalls and crowds, a twin to Petticoat Lane, but with all its senses tuned to a minor key.

At its saturated, noisy core of loudly smelling street food was a dancing bar, European post-war poverty dressed up to go to town, a jewel in the market's rank crown. *Au Metro* is now sadly gone. The text below is an attempt to conjure it back, to resurrect its magnificent strangeness. This nibble of manuscript became the shabby heart of my story *Earwig*, published this year and soon to be made into a movie directed by the visionary Lucile Hadžihalilović. She's asked me to be in it, a cameo as the bar owner of *Au Metro*, serving up drinks to the ghosts of memory.

When God gave the first humans consciousness, he whispered advice under his celestial breath as they shivered their way out of Eden: 'Obscure Thyselves'. Every half-simian with enough ingenuity has since learned to brew or distil fluids and vapours to relieve themselves of the intolerable jabber of thought from time to time, to smudge judgement and nerve.

A good bar is a sanctum to this need. *Au Metro* was a cathedral. These days the shabby cave is gutted, degraded into a fourth-hand furniture shop. Peeling Ricard labels and disconnected light fittings mark the former perimeters of its noise, the dance music of a flea market.

Using bankruptcy like spit to polish the once-expensive tone of its grand boulevards, Liège had in the days I visited it maintained dignity on the rim of its poverty. This had been the armaments centre of Europe for hundreds of years, before the cordite drained to the east. But when I was a regular at *Au Metro*, objects and voices pawed each other, swelling the smells of human meeting, and, as always, a gritty pearl was compressed by such life. *Au Metro* was a transmutation hutch where fiction grew in direct proportion to the dwindling of fact. Alice and the Red Queen could *petit déjeuner* here, their prime ugliness and alienation relished.

The first dance began at eight-thirty. By ten, the over-enthusiastic, the horizontal, and the jabbering harmonica player were being gently shovelled outside. *Au Metro* was not big enough for a stage or a pit, but it did have a shelf. The hunched musicians were folded under the ceiling with their instruments. Their crabbed sway and pulse animated the *demi-mondaine* below: the children, old men and even policemen who couldn't resist the music's charm. They danced like puppets and crashed inside its cramped walls and around the exhausted tables of drinkers. The staff who served them included a six-foot trans-sexual, who beamed down on them, whose stubble splintered the pancake, her milk-blind eye reflected in the next glass of pastis. Her companion was even older, an ink-wash of a lounge toad starched with Dracularian elegance. His ancient white hair was dubbed into negative, a blue-black trickle sometimes sliding down under the arm of his heavily tinted spectacles. Their ornate humanity guided, served and protected the customers with wisdom and humour.

Miraculous things were made in *Au Metro*. It kept strange, split lives that outside would be violently mopped up, cleaned away. *Au Metro* was a place where obscurity was toasted, praised and protected. When it closed in the early nineties obsessive uniformity wielded its broom against the beauty of abnormal growth.

We must conserve nutrient beds of night soil and decay like *Au Metro* in the hope that extraordinary human life might grow there, wondrous, dark foibles in their uncultured digestive skins.

Brian Catling, *A drinker*.

LOVE AT FIRST SIGHT

BLISS WAS IT IN THAT DAWN

Margaret Drabble

I fell in love with Europe on my first visit to Paris, on a school journey when I was seventeen. We were all studying French A-Level, and our organised trip included several nights in a *lycée* near the Panthéon, lectures in French on Corneille and Racine, guided sightseeing, and free time. I loved every moment of it, from the blustery Channel crossing to the hard mattresses and the garlic sausage and the *Winged Victory* at the Louvre. We had never tasted garlic and some of us hated it but I have been enjoying it ever since. It was a week of such revelation and such intensity. I can't describe how moved I was by the Louvre, by the Sainte Chappelle, by the bookshops along the Seine where we bought postcards, by Notre Dame, by the Luxembourg Gardens and the Boulevard St Michel. I had read about these places, and there they were, even more wonderful than I had imagined. Some areas were out of bounds, so of course on our first free evening we headed straight for forbidden Montmartre, and saw a production of Sartre's *Huis Clos*, in a tiny theatre-in-the-round. I can't imagine now how we found out that it was on and managed to buy tickets, as we weren't supposed to be there at all, and nobody can have told us about it. Not all our activities were as highbrow: we visited *La Samaritaine*, where we had a memorable iced coffee, and we also went window shopping on the Champs-Elysées, where we made out to the ultra-chic saleswoman in a very grand store that we were going to buy some Chanel Number Five for our mothers, which none of us could possibly have afforded. Paris was wonderful in every way and I was hooked.

My next visit was also allegedly educational, for I was lucky enough to spend three months of my gap year in Perugia, learning Italian at the *Università per Stranieri*. Again, I found myself in a paradise, this time of pasta and cheap wine and artichokes and architecture, with the thrill of a new language and a whole new literature. The landscapes of Umbria were classic and enchanting, and we toured them and their art galleries by coach. I had never been invited to look at paintings and buildings before, and hardly knew the names of Giotto and Piero della Francesca. Those months laid down the foundation of a lifelong love of Italy, in all its aspects – its food, its language, its art, its monuments, its fountains, its cafes, its culture.

I returned to England immeasurably enriched, and with new eyes for my own country. I started to visit art galleries and churches, and discovered that we too had grand cathedrals and great painters. Over more than sixty years I have had great pleasure from my holidays in and working visits to Europe: France and Italy remain my first and greatest loves, but I also have strong memories of many other European countries. I try to travel by train, as I did when I was seventeen, and am still as uplifted as then I was by the sight of those great trees hung with mistletoe between Calais and Paris, by the Alps seen in the first light of morning from the window of a sleeper. And I am also always moved by returning home, by the sight of the oasthouses and green fields of Kent, by the beauty of the English countryside. Love of Europe deepens one's love of England. How fortunate we are, to be so closely linked, to be so near to so many sublime and subtle differences.

BERLIN: PRESENT FROM THE PAST

Jamie Buxton

I was six when I fell for Berlin and it was an odd affair. My father, a diplomat, was posted there in 1964 – his last posting before a brain tumour killed him. His title was Head of the External Department of the British Military Government, which involved some diplomacy but rather more intelligence work. Sir Peter Hayman, top MI6 spook and later named in the House of Commons as a paedophile, was his boss. I'm slightly disturbed to remember Sir Peter only as a jovial, likeable man who called me Old Buffo and taught me how to fish in the lake behind his house.

We were a family of six: a unit that the posting broke up. My two older sisters were packed off to boarding school, while the youngest one and I went to the British army school. We shopped mostly at the NAAFI, saw other British families, and in the scorching, dusty continental summers spent day after day at the Officer's Club swimming pool. Truth be told, we didn't have much to do with Berliners, but for eighteen darkly vivid months we had a great deal to do with Berlin. The city defined both what we did and who we were in a way that was utterly new to a six-year-old from the quiet London suburb of Blackheath.

I am looking at my father's old ID card as I write this. It is made of orange card and has a prominent Union Jack on the front. Under that is a number: Card no. 338, and then the flowing signature of Major General Peel Yates, General Officer Commanding Berlin – British Sector. Everything is in four languages: English, French, Russian and German. Inside is my father's photograph showing him to be a handsome man, but knowingly careless of such trifles: his hair is messy, his tie skew-whiff, but his eyebrows are slightly cocked and his eyes narrowed. From the letters of condolence that my mother kept, I have learned that he was brilliant at his job but confusingly direct – confusing, that is, to more Machiavellian colleagues. Cocktail parties put him in a muck sweat but his staff loved him. In the Second World War, he was a captain in the Signals and, from what I can gather, operated behind enemy lines in Burma. My eldest sister thinks he had PTSD. As children we were encouraged to be as cheerful, adventurous and uncomplaining as he was, but his temper, when we complained or disobeyed him, could be volcanic. He was a spanker and a shaker.

All this from a fifty-five-year-old card . . .

We were all given these cards, my sisters and I, before we left England with the strict instructions that we were expected to be representational. The chance to show off put me into a small frenzy: I would make sure that Berlin, whatever it was, would be well and truly represented to.

Our Berlin, West Berlin, was defined by the Wall and the Wall was the Cold War made manifest. Where West Berlin met the East German countryside, there was a barbed-wire fence, like something out of *The Great Escape*, and a deceptively innocent-looking strip of grass (it was sown with mines). But the old city centre was broken in half by an eight-foot breeze-block barrier, topped with barbed wire and overlooked by empty tenements. A scant three years old when we arrived, it looked slipshod and flimsy. It was hung with wreaths commemorating East Berliners who had been shot trying to escape to the West. I viewed these with representational solemnity but never really understood what they meant because the Wall, oddly, was not a barrier for us.

My father's diplomatic privileges meant he could pass into the East whenever he wanted, and take his family with him. Checkpoint Charlie was a thrill at first, but soon just a gateway to what became quite familiar outings: to the zoo, to the Pergamon museum, and to the countryside where farmers still ploughed the sandy soil with horses. There was ice cream – red, of course – and far more bombed-out ruins than in the West. Fewer cars and fewer people. Once, my sisters and I were driven there by a colleague of my father's in his Jaguar saloon. We attracted crowds and I felt exclusive, special and set apart. I am afraid that this probably watered the green shoots of love.

The West was different. The bombed-out tenements had been demolished and the rubble piled into a mound, hundreds of feet high, which was topped by an American radar dome, as round and white as a puffball. The bubble on the rubble, we called it. We lived in the unbombed and peaceful suburb of Charlottenburg, near my father's office in the admin buildings of the old Olympic stadium. It was, in retrospect, still haunted by the past – verdigris streaks and old boltholes on the ceremonial pylons showed where bronze eagles and swastikas had once hung – but to me the stadium looked far more impressive than anything shabby old London could offer, ditto the breadth and straightness of the grand city boulevards; ditto the low, wide Mercedes taxis; ditto even the wheelie bins we put our rubbish in – so different, so much more modern than the old metal bins back in England. At Tempelhof airport, the automatic doors slid open, briskly, as you approached. On the boulevards you might see tanks roaring slowly down the road, eating up the tarmac with their tracks. Soldiers carried machine guns, Russian Migs swooped low over the city to break the sound barrier, just to annoy us. Savage that I was, I loved everything about it.

Of course, there are many good reasons to love a city, and Berlin offers more than most. You can love her for her night life, her terrifying cycle lanes, her practical civility, for inspiring David Bowie. You can love her decadent past, her seductive narrative of fall and redemption, her practical drive to mend her broken stones, stagger to her feet and stand, as she does now as the new capital of a new Germany.

But my love is driven by different chemistry, rather sweet and very strange. I have an absolute and distinct memory of my father, the spy with a brain tumour, taking me to see *Funeral in Berlin*, in Berlin. I remember vividly drinking in the delicious grot of the film – the blackened facades of the buildings, the advertising pillars plastered with faded posters – and then the real cityscape mapping itself onto what I had just experienced in the cinema. It's a completely false memory. The film came out a good year after my father had died. Berlin had performed some weird healing magic on my brain, had created significance out of nothing more than a wish.

In Berlin I felt abroad, and not abroad. We were away, but very much at home in our nice British sector. These contradictions were disruptive and formative: they taught me about opposites and for me, today, Berlin combines the dark fascination of Boo Radley's house with the dazzle of the City on the Hill – either Jerusalem or Oz. It makes the perfect frame for my father and his contradictions: containing my memories of him and giving them shape. It also holds my love for him, gives it a place to live and quest, like a small inquisitive zoo animal bumbling around its pen. Berlin was the place that taught me that that security is illusory, memories are what you make them and imagination, like a dream, grows best in the dark.

MY LOVE AFFAIR WITH EUROPE

Deborah Moggach

In the old days, if you were a toff, you went on the Grand Tour. With servants, trunks and chaperones in tow, you'd visit all the great art galleries and museums in Europe, a journey that took several months, and would return a cultivated human being loaded with treasures for your mansion in Belgravia and your country pile.

My own Grand Tour was somewhat different. In 1962, when I was thirteen, I trundled around Europe for three weeks in an old army lorry with a bunch of boys from Watford Grammar School. There were just three of us girls in a lorryload of testosterone, so it was a headily hormonal voyage as well as a cultural one.

It was appallingly uncomfortable. The lorry had no springs. We sat on hard wooden benches facing each other, and when it rained the cover was pulled down and we could see nothing at all. We stayed at campsites and, as far as I can remember, only once ate at a restaurant. It was in Italy and the teacher showed us how to cut up spaghetti into tiny pieces with a knife and fork, and then use a spoon to shovel it in – 'that's how Italians eat it,' he said. The rest of the time it was tinned pilchards, day after day. Such was our gastronomic education.

Ah, but the trip was wonderful. During the three weeks, we drove through Belgium, Holland, Germany, Switzerland, Italy,

Spain and France. We visited cathedrals and churches, museums and galleries. I had always loved art and now found myself standing in front of paintings by Dürer, Memling, Fra Angelico, Giotto, Leonardo da Vinci, Bosch. Heart hammering, I gazed at frescoes that were thrillingly brought to life by the insertion of a coin. We must have been shuffling around together, but I can't remember that. My spotty companions fell away and I was alone, wandering ancient streets, footsteps echoing, bells tolling, my breath stopped by the sudden sight of a statue or the glorious facade of a church. Intoxicating cooking smells drifted out from restaurants. Chic people sat in cafes drinking espressos and wine, both unheard of in my drab suburban world. This was civilisation. Even now, over fifty years later, I still can feel the rush of joy from an experience that changed my life.

So I'm forever grateful to Watford Grammar School for opening my eyes to the wonderment that existed across the Channel. It started my lifelong love affair with Europe, particularly France and Italy. Needless to say, I've been there countless times thanks to the marvellous Eurostar, which can take you to Paris for lunch. Since the seventies I've even had a shared, tiny house in the Lot valley (shared with twelve others) where I've swum in the river and eaten memorable meals.

I also have a special love for Amsterdam. I wrote a novel set there, called *Tulip Fever*. It was a romantic drama played out during the weird period of tulipmania, in 1637, and was bought by Steven Spielberg and made into a film. I also adapted *Anne Frank's Diary* for the BBC, which sent me back to the city and was a hugely emotional experience.

I've always considered myself a European, rather than a Brit. Europe has given me culture, a liberal sensibility, and a richness beyond words. And it all started back in the fifties, among a gaggle of schoolboys from Watford who'll be grandfathers now. I hope it had such a transformative effect on them. I suspect it did.

LIKE A PFUCKKING TAART!

Holly Johnson

My childhood memories are like a black-and-white kitchen-sink drama set in Liverpool in the sixties. Back-to-back terraced houses, a bedroom with Beatles wallpaper. John, Paul, George and Ringo staring down smiling, back from their residency in Hamburg where they wore leather jackets and mixed with the arty set.

I was a child interested in a world heard on the radio and seen on television: *Dr Who*, *Top of the Pops*, *A Magical Mystery Tour*, and *Sgt Pepper's Lonely Hearts Club Band* on the portable record player.

Then there was Saturday morning cinema: Elvis, Holy Technicolor BATMAN! And just like Dorothy when her house landed in Munchkinland, I experienced the world turning all the colours of the rainbow: Gene Kelly in *An American in Paris*, singing 'I got rhythm, I got music . . .' Yes, Paris.

I was led through the portal of pop music by child catchers Marc Bolan and David Bowie into a parallel universe. Marc had met an inspirational Frenchman, a wizard. I devoured his slim volume of poetry *The Warlock of Love*. Then songs by Jacques Brel, the Belgian songwriter, were covered by Bowie. 'Amsterdam' and 'My Death' transported me. Bowie's seven-inch single called 'Jean Genie' played on the name Jean Genet. I was fascinated by

Lindsay Kemp too, teacher of movement and mime to Bowie and later Kate Bush. He created *Flowers*, a theatrical interpretation of Genet's novel *Our Lady of the Flowers*. Championed by Jean Cocteau and given sainthood and martyrdom by Jean-Paul Sartre, Genet was my idol and his art of the underworld captured my imagination.

And it was to Paris I went on the boat-train, a hovercraft in fact, when I first visited Europe at eighteen, wearing a leather Muir cap à la Tom of Finland and then buying a round sailors' or 'Marine' hat, feeling like Querelle of Brest as I walked the Rue Saint-Denis near the Beaubourg, where glamorous street walkers strutted in high heels, theatrical makeup, leotards and fishnet stockings in broad daylight. Meanwhile military police carrying machine guns lined up in formation on busy shopping boule-vards, and nearby bikers in leather gathered around the Bastille. I stayed with friends of a friend on the Boulevard Beaumarchais, a stone's throw from the Jewish quarter, where I removed my leather peaked cap out of respect to those who had lost their lives.

We dined at Chatier (Bouillon Chatier), a famously cheap and cheerful brasserie for students, workers and starving artists like myself. In the *Belle Époque* dining room, the waistcoated waiter wrote out the bill on the disposable tablecloth.

Paris was a gateway drug for me, leading to each and every capital I could reach on the *Trans-Europe Express*. Europe came into my life in this electronic musical ode to the train by Kraftwerk, Germany's pioneering electro-pop stars. 'Meet Iggy Pop and David Bowie' rang through the speakers in *les discotheques*.

Along with Lou Reed, Iggy and Bowie were adored by my

generation, as a cult of cool, both hanging out with Romy Haag, the Dutch trans-fabulous singer and songwriter who had her own nightclub. Romance ensued, and Romy and Bowie were photographed seated at a table and kissing, Bowie still beautiful though emaciated from his LA cocaine addiction. He stayed near to one of Christopher Isherwood's Berlin flats, and both now sport commemorative plaques (at Nollendorfstrasse 17 and Haupstrasse 155). Isherwood wrote *Goodbye to Berlin* in that street. In the eventual play, musical, film adaptation *Cabaret*, 'Divine Decadence Darling' was played out in the Kit Kat Club by Liza Minnelli and Joel Grey. This dramatisation of the prelude to the century's worst atrocities echoed down the decades. In 1976 Bowie arrived back in the UK to give what looked like a Nazi salute from the back of his hired Mercedes Benz 600 Pullman Landaulette Limousine.

A few years later in an Amsterdam leather bar I met an ex-pat Liverpudlian who had once lived in a respectable row of Georgian houses near Gambier Terrace, last seen brushing his doorstep with a woman's frilly pinafore over his office attire. He turned to me as a huge muscled man descended into the dark back room where we were standing.

'She's off her head that one. Have you taken a pill?'

'No,' I replied, feeling quite the country bumpkin.

He fumbled about in his leather chaps, produced a red capsule and proclaimed: 'Here you are, love. You're a bit rough and ready . . . but you'll do.'

I woke up on a houseboat on a canal with a large Elvis impersonator on top of me.

'It was the only polite way to wake you up,' he explained.

'You look like a pfuckking taart!' I remembered what my father used to yell at me as I exited our terraced house in the mornings, my hair teased into an approximation of Marc Bolan's corkscrew coiffure.

Now in Amsterdam I could smile at that. And even sympathise. 'What 'av I done to deserve a freak-show for a son?'

What indeed?

The revelation that one ate chips (bought at vendors on the street) with MAYONNAISE impressed me more than all the paintings in the Van Gogh Museum. It was in Amsterdam that I saw the Baltimore Bombshell Divine perform in and out of drag. All of this seemed impossibly glamorous to a boy from Liverpool. England was like a stay-at-home suburban housewife while Europe was a mistress encrusted with jewels in her boudoir, a Picasso hanging on the wall and reflected in the mirror of her dressing table, while she sprays herself with an exotic perfume by Schiaparelli, the bottle designed by a surrealist. She is late for an assignation. Maybe at the Opera where Maria Callas sings or an opening night for the *Ballet Russe* with Nijinsky, or Josephine Baker and Grace Jones dancing together into the night. *La Belle et La Bête* flickers on a cinema screen. Marlene Dietrich sings Lilli Marlene in *The Blue Angel*. Anne Frank writes an entry in her diary. An Italian Futurist poet spills his absinthe and the Green Fairy flies away. Do not forget, Europa, we love you.

EVERY CLOUD . . .

Isy Suttie

Travelling back from Australia in the spring of 2010, ensconced in a soft nest of Iris Murdoch and Maltesers, my plane was an hour or so away from London when the pilot's voice came over the tannoy. 'Ladies and gentlemen, due to the ash cloud our route has been diverted.' A low-level panic set in among my fellow passengers. Diverted? 'We're not going to die . . .' he continued calmly, 'but we *are* going to France.'

That night, after hours stationary on the runway while the airline tried to find us rooms for the night, I chastised myself for not paying more attention to the news when I'd been at the Melbourne Comedy Festival. This so-called ash cloud, which had sounded like nothing more than something Dot Cotton might have to contend with, had spewed out of an Icelandic volcano and was wreaking havoc on flights throughout Europe. And so I found myself lying alone – mercifully – in a twin room in a Mexican-themed hotel at the edge of Eurodisney, with no way of knowing how long this would go on for. 'Keep coming back and checking with us, *madame et monsieur*,' they'd say as we all repeatedly asked reception how and when we would get home. 'Do not leave the hotel. We will not telephone individuals.'

I'd previously been to Paris for a few brief visits, and found myself very much the peasant girl pressing her nose against the window of the big house, without completely comprehending the riches she was looking at, and secretly wishing she was scrumping apples from the orchard instead. But now it didn't feel like we were even *in* Paris. We were marooned in a Disney Mexico where muzak played constantly and everyone ate far too much unyielding bread.

Other people from the flight (that is, most of us in the hotel) had serious problems to contend with – much more serious than mine. At breakfast after a jetlagged first night I sat eating Mexican-themed croissants with an elderly couple who were about to run out of their medication. A young girl with her mum was missing her dad in England. All I was missing was a gig in Reading and my boyfriend back in Australia.

Nevertheless, I decided it was time to take immediate action. I managed to corral anyone who was travelling alone and looked like they could do with getting away from the hand-drawn pictures of Goofy, and perhaps towards *un pastis*. By lunchtime about seven or eight of us had, against reception's insistence, abandoned the hotel for Paris itself. In our intrepid group of solo travellers we had a paramedic and a surgeon, plus a guy who was supposed to be the best man at a wedding in Scotland the next day. He was figuring out how to film his speech because he didn't expect to make it. The bizarre nature of the situation made us much more open and frank than we would have been ordinarily. Almost immediately a woman started telling me all about her toxic relationship with her mother.

We started drinking as soon as we came off the metro, in one of those cafes that are ten a penny in Paris – often on a corner, with big windows and lots of brass inside. Without having thought about it I had entered the big house, and was knocking back the riches like there was no tomorrow. Bubbling with something close to blissful hysteria at times, we bought and shared cigarettes and croque monsieurs and tall glasses of beer. What would happen when our naughty group got back to the hotel? Would we be stuck here for ever? Paris felt so exciting to me, perhaps because I was with the right group of people, giddy with jetlag and *joie de vivre*.

We studied the Eiffel Tower and Notre Dame and I took in their true, honest majesty for the first time, linking arms with the others and discussing the difficulty of paramedics' hours and work.

Somehow, Paris being the backdrop to all this drama was perfect. It was foreign, of course, but utterly familiar; a place I had completely taken for granted until now. 'The beer is ice cold!' I thought. 'The architecture! The scarves! *Les poubelles*!' Before, I'd simply tried too hard, attempting to woo Paris, to find its heart, to dress like its women. It turned out that, for me, Paris was like the sun: if I didn't look directly at it, it would light my way.

By nightfall we were en route back to the hotel for a brief shower and change before heading to a nightclub we'd spotted near Notre Dame. On entering reception we saw pinned to the front desk a handwritten sign saying a coach was on its way from England and we'd be leaving at 2.45am. My heart sank as we secreted satsumas and biscuits in serviettes for the journey.

We tried to have a reunion exactly a year later at Trafalgar Square, but it was raining and just wrong. 'But we'll always have Paris,' I thought on the way home, and this was true, and it was enough.

A STUDENT CHRISTMAS IN PARIS

Kathleen Burk

In September 1970, I arrived from California to take up a place as a history undergraduate at Oxford. I settled in very well, but as Christmas approached and I realised all my friends were planning to go home to their families, I decided to go to Paris. I went by myself – in those days, students tended not to worry too much about safety. In any case, I was fast and strong, and knew that I could take care of myself. I hitched to the ferry and travelled to France standing in a crowded, rolling ship, continuing thence to Paris on a very slow bus. Wearing my backpack and carrying a guitar, I had enough money with me to pay for a few nights in a youth hostel situated on the edge of the city. I could also eat frugally, depending on an occasional omelette au jambon or a pot of yoghurt and a bread roll for sustenance.

On the evening before Christmas Eve, I wandered to the Quartier Latin, where I found a group of students and joined them. I do not remember where we sat, nor what our little area looked like: I was just delighted to be on that fabled ground. It was not very cold, so there was no excuse to snuggle. We played guitars and sang Bob Dylan songs, that I knew, and French songs, that I didn't, sharing stuffed pitta breads and 15p-a-litre red wine that we had bought from the little shops lining the streets. The aroma of the meat in the pitta breads mingled with the smell of the drains to produce a scent that I will always associate with that evening. As the night wore on, more and more students joined us. Wandering around and chatting, I found that most of them had been hitching around Europe and were flowing into Paris for Christmas from Madrid, Berlin, Rome and elsewhere. That night was the first time that I felt part of a community in Europe. Since then, I have never again lived in America.

FRANÇOISE

Paul Atterbury

'*Tu veux?*' I looked up and into the smiling eyes of a pretty red-haired girl who took my hand and led me into the dancing throng of French teenagers. It was a dance at the *lycée* in Paris where I was spending a month with a group from my London school, and most of us were standing around on the edge of the throng, just watching.

She pulled me closer and put her arms around me. '*Je m'appelle Françoise, Françoise Brouillard*, like the fog, *tu sais*, in England.' We danced on, not saying much, and then she took me away into a quieter, darker corner. She kissed me. It was everything I had thought about endlessly as I walked the Parisian streets, watching French girls passing. And here was one of those girls, in my arms, and wanting to be kissed. The evening passed, and in between kisses we talked about everything. Finally, it was time to go home. We met again the next day, after school, and walked along beside the Seine, talking, kissing and laughing. Suddenly, I knew I had grown up. A couple of days later the school exchange was over.

Françoise was funny, clever, lovely, gently sexy, delightful to be with and quite sophisticated in a completely French way. I know now that I owe Françoise, and France, a great debt. She shaped my life by introducing me to the many pleasures of female company, something that at the time I knew nothing about but have since enjoyed for sixty years. There were a few letters but we never met again.

SHARING TIME

Zoë Beaty

The man who greeted us when we arrived appeared to have painted his skin a glossy orange emulsion that matched the dip-dyed 'sunrise' cocktail in his hand. He said hello, and *hola*, and looked at my mum's magnolia arm next to his. The whole world was in a brochure on his table, he told my parents. We had made it here, to Tenerife, where raging volcanoes and dolphins live; the rest was for the taking. He was selling Time – one week, each year, for a small price. When he wasn't looking, I stole the glittering fan perched in his drink and put it in my bumbag with the fancy paper coaster off the plane.

We had travelled in economy in a class still a bit too posh for families like ours. I had raced raindrops down the window of our Austin Montego all the way to the airport, taking bets on the raindrops in the left and right corners to see which would fall fastest. If I won the bet, we were about to see mermaids in the place I'd been told was a long way from Cleethorpes. After my parents signed the man's paper, I repeated the betting ritual the next year, too, and the year after that.

Most years then, for one week, we went to see the world of Tenerife. We howled at the man on keyboards impersonating Elton John each night and begged for his CD and were mesmerised by the poolside 'fashion show' (you could buy a sarong) and the way the pool glowed bright neon at night-time and lusted after 'hairwraps' and scaled the snoozing volcano and bought porcelain dolphins, carefully transported back to reality, and I grew an inch or more each time. I swam under the water until I gave up on mermaids and made friends instead; older friends, friends with funny accents and one as tall as me and with even bigger feet. Later, I stole pesetas 'for the pool table', which we guiltily fed to the Budweiser vending machine around the corner until we vomited and lashed our tongues in the mouths of boys our parents didn't know about. They vomited too.

Just over a decade passed until Time ran out and some of the men selling it appeared in headlines – fraud and 'aggressive tactics' and owners of Time being kept inside it 'under duress'. 'Timeshare fees: trapped in a holiday that lasts a lifetime', the *Telegraph* said. The thing is, it did, and the thing is, I always won the bet.

OUR HORIZONS ARE NEVER CLOSED

Lee Rourke

I first saw Europe from the sky. From the cockpit of a Dan Air 727 en route to Mallorca. It was our first holiday outside of the UK. I was seven years old. I'd never really thought about Europe up until that holiday. Through my love of football, I knew some of the countries, but other than the odd European Cup discussion or school test, Europe meant very little to me.

This all changed 35,000 feet up in the air. I remember the take-off being electrifying, literally, as we lifted upwards through the thunderstorm that was circling Manchester. I remember being upset that there was so much cloud I couldn't see anything as I strained my neck to peer out through the small window. Then, about an hour into the flight, a member of the cabin crew came over to us and asked my parents if I would like to join the captain and co-pilot in the cockpit. I jumped at the chance; it was this plane-spotting child's dream.

The first thing that struck me as I was ushered through the unlocked door was how laid-back the captain and co-pilot were, both facing each other, casually chatting, one of them drinking tea. The light outside was crepuscular and the cockpit's dials and switches were lit up like jewels. When I looked out of the window, the clouds had disappeared.

'Wow, what's that?' I remember asking.

'It's the Pyrenees,' the captain replied in a matter-of-fact tone. 'Directly below us is France, and just past those peaks is the Iberian Peninsula – the rest of Europe is behind us now . . .'

I stood transfixed. I didn't know what to say. All of the geeky aviation questions I'd been thinking about asking disappeared as my eyes, unblinking, stared into the magical view ahead. I remember not being able to fully compute what I was seeing. It looked like a painting. It was a masterpiece.

'It's beautiful down there, isn't it?' the captain said, still in that matter-of-fact tone.

'Yes,' I mumbled, 'it is.'

I don't want to ruin the picture I have in my head. No simile or metaphor or adjective could do it justice. I just want to see the Pyrenees as I did that day, as I've seen them every time I've flown that way in the intervening years: *truly* beautiful.

Whenever someone mentions the word 'Europe', be it with friends, or on the news, that image, the beautiful image of the Pyrenees, from 35,000 feet up in the air, comes back to me. I would never want to be disconnected from this image; it represents a special time when I began to look past the horizons of my own life into new worlds and cultures. I would never want to feel separated from Europe. Never. Europe has always been a gateway for me, and I've always felt that it's part of my life.

READING THE COFFEE GROUNDS

Philip Carr-Gomm

Love seems to work best when we cannot fully understand what is going on – that delicious sense of mystery, of irrationality. My falling in love with Sofia was like that – drawn to the shabby chic of the buildings, the complete lack of 'customer care', the simplicity of the food, the warmth of the people once you gained their trust. And from that first visit in 1974 the love grew, and I would go every spring, when the cherry blossom filled the streets, and Mt Vitosha shone white with snow on the horizon. And I would go with my friends on the ski-lift up on to the mountain and look down on the city, or I would sit in the crypt of the Alexander Nevsky cathedral bathing in the golden glow of its icons.

It was all *impossibly* 'Other' – so near to Europe and yet so different: the Iron Curtain, the sullen policemen, the stories of life under the dictator Todor Zhivkov. Drawn to this strangeness, flirting with learning the language, even with eventually living there, I got closer to a world of people yearning for Western free-doms, but also often loyal to their Russian friends who had saved them from 600 years of Turkish domination.

The darkness of this world that I had been enjoying as a visi-tor, amused and intrigued by its otherness, reared its head brutally when a friend was suddenly arrested in the summer of

1981. Months later, the doorbell of his apartment rang, and his wife and daughter were handed his clothes by a soldier. On the top of this neatly folded pile was one bullet, the one that had been used to execute him as a 'traitor'.

At that time it seemed impossible that the regime in Bulgaria would ever change. But it did, in 1989, and since 2007 it has been a member of the European Union – not freed of all its problems, but freed of the repression of a regime that killed its detractors.

The Bulgarians have a long tradition of mysticism. It was here that the Bogomils, precursors of the Cathars, challenged the theology of Constantinople. It is in its southern mountains that the ancient city of Perperikon, the 'Machu Picchu of Europe', lays claim to being the legendary Oracle of Dionysus. And still today the Bulgarians' passion for the mystical can be found in their love of another kind of oracle: reading the coffee grounds.

And so, when I drink a Turkish coffee on the streets of Sofia, and eat a *banitsa* – a national delicacy, a sort of croissant made with feta – I can look up at the cherry blossom and further on to the snow on Mt Vitosha, and still enjoy the uniqueness, the otherness of this place. But I can also do something I couldn't do before: I can enjoy the feeling that the people here are at last free, and are part of the wider community that is Europe today. And I can look down into the coffee grounds in my empty cup and try to divine the future of my own divided country, caught as it is between dreams of past greatness and the fear of irrevocable loss.

MALTA MADE ME

Roger Crowley

July 1960. Aged nine, I am a hopelessly overdressed English schoolboy standing on the tarmac of Luqa airport, experiencing the full blast of Mediterranean heat for the first time. My father is a naval officer stationed on Malta and my brother and I are here for the summer holidays.

Those two months shaped my life. Malta was overwhelming: the light, the smell of dust, the bleached limestone landscape, the small fields hedged with prickly pears. We drank a lot of 7up, hummed along to some song about yellow polka-dot bikinis and swam in the local rock-cut bathing pools where I caught impetigo. We pottered around the island on my dad's naval launch, put in at secluded coves and jumped clean into the bluest seas. At night I fell asleep quickly – the last thing I remembered was the scent of smouldering Tiger Coils to ward off mosquitoes.

On Malta I absorbed both history and pre-history. With my mother we visited extraordinary megalithic monuments, descended into the eerie underground Neolithic temple of the Hypogeum, scrambled over the ramparts of Valletta in the wake of the Knights of St John. On a beach we found pointed sharks' teeth, as shiny as new. Back in England we took them to the Natural History Museum. They were twenty million years old. My mind was made up: I was no longer going to be a naval officer; I would dig into the earth, become an archaeologist.

Somehow that never quite happened. The ancient past escaped me. It was too far away, too hard to imagine. I wanted to hear human voices – the Knights defending Malta against the Ottomans proved more compelling than the megaliths. Either way, this first contact with the Mediterranean proved decisive. I have returned often not just to travel but to write about the history of Europe's presence in a sea of ideas that binds us all.

THE MOLO AUDACE

Beth Lynch

At this time of day, the light diminishing, the stone expanse
seems infinite. It stretches pale out to sea, into the closing atmosphere. The sun will set soon.

It is not yet dinner-time in Trieste and the pier, the Molo
Audace, is crowded, chattering. Italian, mainly, and a Slavic
language that I cannot grasp. I tune into fragments of German
conversation. There are snatches of French, American English
and who knows what else in the collective hum.

Everyone is out and about, local and transient, old and young
– but despite the crowd the pier does not feel busy. This place is
inimical to haste. Unless you are a small child or jockeying teenager, the Molo Audace slows your pace and obliges you to
wander, amble, thread your way, as we are doing now. A man is
sitting barefoot on one edge, his suit trousers rolled up as if by
habit though the water is far out of reach. Someone is playing a
guitar. There are people with dawdling or hurtling children,
people bumping into people they know, people with chunky
cameras and the air of visitors. A small gathering around a
ghetto blaster, an elderly woman perched on a mooring bollard.
Her back is ramrod straight and her look faraway.

A brightening of the sky, resolving forms and figures into
crisp silhouettes. Out in the Adriatic a cargo ship is inching

from Western to Eastern Europe – Venice, most likely, to somewhere in Croatia. Here we are neither west nor east. This sliver of Italy trails south-eastward, sandwiched between Slovenia and the sea, appended to the one country and anchored in the other. Once the great seaport of the Austro-Hungarian Empire, Trieste was annexed by Italy after the First World War and saw its share of totalitarian darkness in the Second. Delicately located on the dividing line of the new 'Iron Curtain', the region was designated a free territory in 1947; it was portioned between Yugoslavia and Italy seven years later, when the city reverted to Italy.

This hybrid of a city. The Habsburg architecture of the Piazza dell'Unità d'Italia. The Canal Grande, redolent of Venice, with the Byzantine bulk of a Serbian Orthodox Church. The Mitteleuropean coffee houses, their faded grandeur; the holes in walls where '*caffè*' means Illy espresso straight up; the functionally tiled bars where beer and Slovenian ham are served forthrightly. The old-town neighbourhoods that are themselves. The street where, much later, we will join a lively queue outside Gelato Marco, and the gelato will be worth the wait.

Trieste is a city with a hinterland, its own place: I love it for this. I love it, too, for the sparseness of tourist attractions: there are no obligations here, nor boxes to tick, so that, however brief your stay, you do not visit the city so much as inhabit it. Most of all I love the Molo Audace: the sea, the collectiveness.

The conversational din has stopped abruptly. Nothing but seagulls, traffic. A protesting child. Everyone is standing, turned to the sea, expectant, and I think of churches and solstices. The sun is setting. It dissolves gold then red into clouds at the horizon, and the silhouetted crowd blurs into dusk, silent still, looking out to sea. Together we have witnessed a marvel, the setting of the sun on a Tuesday in September.

I turn around and look back to the city. A full moon is rising and has paused perfectly above the Greek Orthodox church. A bright orb centred on a starry metal cross. I take a photograph, then put my camera away. When I look up again, the moon is off-centre and the sky is the colour of dusk on a clear evening, neither blue nor grey.

LET ME COUNT THE WAYS

COUPS DE FOUDRE

Hermione Lee

13 ways of falling in love with Europe (from the ages of 7 to 70)

1. A silver dish of tiny wild strawberries, on a table of heavy white linen in an old-fashioned restaurant in Bordeaux in 1955.
2. Carlo Maria Giulini conducting Rossini's *The Barber of Seville* at Covent Garden in 1960.
3. The windows of Chartres at dusk.
4. The party in the magical house in Alain Fournier's *Le Grand Meaulnes*, a paradise of delicate elegant joy and excited children, in a place you may never find again.
5. Trumpets of the end of time sounding from a distance, getting closer ('Tuba mirum'), in Verdi's *Requiem*.
6. Artichoke risotto in a small restaurant in Trastevere in Rome, eaten in the 1980s with my life's companion.
7. The Unicorn Tapestries, from fifteenth- and sixteenth-century Brussels and Paris, by way of Rockefeller in 1922, in joyous captivity in the Cloisters in New York.
8. Strauss's song *Morgen!*: 'And tomorrow the sun will shine again . . . and silently we will look in each other's eyes / and on us will sink the mute silence of happiness . . .'
9. The amphitheatre at Delphi, ringed by Mount Parnassos and the Peloponnese.

10. Seurat's *Bathers at Agnières*, the painting I always wanted to be taken to in the National Gallery as a child; ordinary people on their day out, patiently sitting by the river in the suburban, industrial landscape, bathed in their golden glow.

11. Mozart's *The Marriage of Figaro*, the greatest of all operas, by an Austrian composer, set in Spain, with an Italian libretto, based on a French play; an opera of revolution, danger, class war, power, love, sex, confusion, comedy and forgiving, for all times and nations.

12. Edith Wharton's Mediterranean view from her garden in Old Hyères, home of a magnificent American novelist in love all her life with France.

13. Beethoven's setting of Schiller's *Ode to Joy* ('Seid umschlungen, Millionen!') in his Ninth Symphony: music of hope, heroism, courage, nobility and common humanity, music not to turn your back on.

ODYSSEY

Tony Robinson

The first book I ever remember reading was about Odysseus and his agonisingly long journey home. Then I encountered Theseus and the Minotaur, Jason and his Fleece, and the other muscle-bound ancient Greek heroes and sometimes vengeful, always long-suffering heroines. I still remember the day I discovered that the Roman gods were rebranded versions of my newfound friends the Greek deities – Venus was Aphrodite, Neptune was Poseidon, Diana was Artemis. Wow! I didn't know why or how it happened, I still don't really, but the discovery was amazing.

In my teens, to the accompaniment of 'I Wanna Hold Your Hand' and wearing a 'Ban the Bomb' badge, I absorbed myself in Camus, Sartre, de Beauvoir and Malraux. They dripped with meaning, although I wasn't quite sure what the meaning was.

At nineteen I played the middle-aged dupe Orgon in Molière's excoriating play *Tartuffe*, my hair plastered with white liquid makeup, and sporting a limp and a stick to indicate my character's advanced years. I worked alongside Donald Sinden in Ibsen's majestic *Enemy of the People*, a play that should be required reading in these dark days.

In my kaftan, and through heavily smudged John Lennon glasses, I read Hermann Hesse, Günter Grass and Thomas Mann. Then Cervantes, Goethe and Dante until in my fifties I finally realised I'd been imbibing far too much testosterone and turned my attention to writers such as Colette and George Sand. I am currently feasting on Elena Ferrante's glorious *My Brilliant Friend* trilogy, both on TV and in book form.

On this odyssey I've never once thought of any of the above authors as exotic, foreign or outside my sphere of understanding. They are as much part of me as Shakespeare, the Brontës and the Beatles. They shaped me, moulded me, wrought me. I am British and I am European. Neither diminishes the other. Both enhance the other.

WHY WE LOVE EUROPE

Richard Overy

Imagine modern culture without Picasso, Dostoevskii, Nietzsche, Matisse, Shostakovich, Brahms, Dali, Gide; and so on. The list is endless and the contribution of the major European artists, writers, thinkers and musicians to shaping British culture is profound, but never acknowledged enough. I have spent my career as a historian writing on subjects that span the flowering of European modernism. This rich legacy unites Britain with the rest of the continent in a shared cultural heritage. Hanging on my walls are Kandinsky, Miró, Magritte (but also Henry Moore); if asked to take one book on a desert island, I would take Nietzsche's *Birth of Tragedy*, one of the great books of the modern age; my love for opera came from watching a performance of Verdi's *Aida* in the open air in Rome many years ago as an impoverished student hitchhiking around Europe. I watched the opera again thirty years later in the round in the Royal Albert Hall, surrounded by others like me happy to relish the richness and diversity of a shared European cultural past. My life has been enriched by engagement with European culture, and so too the lives of millions of others. Art, literature and music transcend political squabbles and social divisions, even wars and revolutions, and long may we continue to applaud and appreciate our common cultural past, present and future.

A PUMA IN EUROPE

David Lindo

I guess this is a letter of love primarily for the billions of flora and fauna that inhabit a continent that we humans have split into at least fifty sovereign states. I cannot write this letter without saying that some of my love is also for the citizens of Europe. Citizens that, by and large, I have found to be friendly and hospitable.

This love affair started a long time ago. Perhaps just a little after my passion for natural history was born. In my previous life I am certain that I was a puma hunting birds as a primary source of nourishment. One day, while stalking a potential meal I accidently cracked a twig underfoot and startled my erstwhile prey. The bird took to the wing with a flurry of flapping, leaving me to marvel at its beauty. From then on I chose to watch birds, bewitched by their grace of flight. I no longer ate, which led to my demise.

So, I came into this world pre-equipped with an innate interest in nature. I grew up in Wembley, north-west London, in a neighbourhood in which nobody shared my passion for natural history that, incidentally, started with a fascination for insects. My mother, a young Jamaican woman who had come to England along with my father to seek a better life, did not understand why her son had such an unrelenting interest in nature. But she indulged my growing curiosity by patiently allowing me to ask her a myriad of questions despite her not knowing the answers. I had an insatiable thirst for knowledge but no mentor. By the age of five, when I discovered birds in my garden, I did not know what they were called so I renamed them. Sparrows were 'baby birds', starlings were 'mummy birds', blackbirds were 'daddy birds' and crows were 'uncle birds'. Looking up, I noted the wood pigeons that during the summer months would engage in their display flights: flapping up into the sky before gliding back down on spread wings. They were duly renamed 'jack-in-the-boxes'.

At the age of seven, I found a bird book in my local library that blew my young mind. It was entitled *Birds of Britain, Europe, North Africa and the Middle East*. For me it was manna from heaven. A book featuring over one thousand species, it documented every bird ever to step foot, glide over or swim past Europe. I religiously read it cover to cover, even during school lessons. Indeed, it led to my classmates calling me Bird Brain because of my all-consuming interest. I was fascinated by the overwhelming variety of birds that the book covered and I particularly focused on the individual distribution maps of the various species. At the time, my knowledge of the countries of Europe was rudimentary, but I was bemused and excited by the notion that some species occurred geographically fairly close to the UK but yet were never recorded here. I did not understand why. I had no concept of the distances involved or the habitats to be found in the other regions of Europe. I did not even realise that Britain had its own geographical place within the continent. There were certain plates in this book that contained species that particularly fascinated me. One such example was the plate that featured the bustards: a family of large turkey-like game birds that stalked the vast sierras of Spain and the grasslands of Eastern Europe. The largest species was the great bustard. I did not understand how such a large bird could be seen in a country that seemed so close to Britain and yet was not found here. Another spread within the book featured the harriers: graceful raptors, the males of which are largely pale grey. This group really captured my imagination. Harriers are named after their habit of quartering grassy landscapes to flush out and harry their prey: small birds. They seemed so widespread on the continent and yet rare and patchily distributed in Britain. Why was that? Did that mean that I had to go to Europe to see them?

It took a while, years in fact, before I realised that Europe was made up of a mosaic of habitats each harbouring wildlife that had adapted to live there over millennia. I have learned that Europe is a significant place for birds. I have explored the continent with all its different cultures and have discovered such remarkably varied landscapes. There are the subtropical coasts of the Mediterranean where African species like the pink and perky Trumpeter finch rub alulae with our more familiar birds such as swallows. Then there are the Alpine mountain ranges where Alpine choughs, a yellow-billed elegant crow, playfully ride the thermals. Along rugged coastal cliffs peregrines rule, and rural pastures from where corncrakes and quail add their distinctive voices to the soundtrack of the countryside. Estuaries stacked with migrating shorebirds who travel to and from their arctic breeding grounds. There are forests that echo with the drumming of woodpeckers and the mellifluous song of nightingales. And then there are our many urban areas that foster populations of robins and black redstarts. In the temperate North where the winters are bleak and unrelenting, white ptarmigan tread the snow. Europe, you are amazing. You are beautiful, surprising, breathtaking and varied. I am truly in love with you. My passion for birds started in Europe and my passion for Europe, I am sure, will never end.

MY EUROPEAN HEROES

Gyles Brandreth

I don't think I have ever really left the happy world I inhabited in the first fifteen years of my existence. My heroes now were my heroes then and, interestingly, apart from Shakespeare and Mr Pastry, I think they are all continental Europeans.

I was born in a British Forces' Hospital in Germany in 1948. My father was a lawyer serving with the Allied Control Commission helping to establish a new legal system in Germany after the war. Bizarrely, when I was a toddler in Germany, my parents engaged a man to look after me. He was my nanny, I suppose, but we didn't call him that. We called him Hans. Before the war, he had been a circus clown and, when I was three or four, he taught me a range of circus skills (I can still walk a tight-rope and stand on my head – truly) and, as a small boy, I became a circus obsessive. My first true hero was a Russian clown called Popov. I had posters of him all over my bedroom wall.

In the early 1950s, my parents returned to England. I spoke fluent German, but since they couldn't find a German school in London, they sent me to the French *lycée* in South Kensington instead. There I discovered new heroes, starting with Joan of Arc (even aged seven I knew I fancied her), Napoleon Bonaparte (at the time no one told me what a monster he was), and Fernandel, a comic actor of genius, with a face like a horse, whose films (notably *Le Petit Monde de don Camillo* and its sequels) have remained lifetime favourites.

At the *lycée* I actually met a living hero (he was almost a living god) when Charles de Gaulle, on a state visit to the United Kingdom, came to the school. I remember his height, his nose, his stomach (his *bidon* as we called it), and his military uniform. Recently, I was shown footage of his visit to the school and it turns out he was wearing a suit, so it seems I imagined the uniform. We dress our heroes as we want to find them.

In my teenage years, I began visiting continental Europe. When I was fourteen, in a Ford Consul, with a cousin (who was eighteen and Canadian), I raced through ten European countries in ten days. Wherever I went I bought books. By then, theatre was my passion. In France, having seen *Cyrano de Bergerac*, still my favourite play, I bought everything by Edmond Rostand I could lay my hands on. In Germany, I bought Brecht. In Switzerland, the complete works of both Friedrich Dürrenmatt and Max Frisch. In Italy, I became a Goldoni groupie; in Spain I devoured the whole of Lope de Vega – at least I felt I did. I can't have done, of course: Lope de Vega is reckoned to have written more than 500 plays.

Beyond Shakespeare (who was English, no question), and Sheridan, Wilde, Shaw and O'Casey (all Irish, of course), the heroes of my adolescence were all continental Europeans: Molière, Stendhal, Chekhov, Ibsen, Strindberg. They still are. Recently I went on an Ibsen holiday, travelling around Norway in the great playwright's footsteps. As I write this, I am just back from a trip to Hans Christian Andersen's birthplace. (He was an odd cove. The Swedish Nightingale, Jenny Lind, was his Joan of Arc.)

My soul belongs to the continental Europe of my childhood. My father died in a hospice with Radio 2 blaring in the background. I shall die happy if as I go I am listening to the songs I first heard in the 1950s: Marlene Dietrich, perhaps, or Tino Rossi, or Charles Trenet. Yes, I will be content to be swept away on a tide of *La Mer*.

Happily, none of this will be affected when the UK leaves the EU. In the 2016 referendum, I voted Remain (of course), but I accepted the result (of course) – just as I accepted the result when the electorate in the city of Chester voted me out of Parliament at the general election in 1997, though, God knows, they were WRONG, WRONG, WRONG. The EU is simply an organisation – a way of doing things. The Europe I love – the Europe that gave birth to all my heroes – will still be there. And open. And free. And mine. (Yours, too, of course.)

IN THE PICTURE

Ben Moor

I'm a boy of nine. I don't know the names of the great European artists of the Renaissance or of any other time. But I do know the names of Carlos Ezquerra, Massimo Belardinelli, Jesus Redondo. They are the European artists on *2000 AD: The Galaxy's Greatest Comic*. Their artwork has action, passion and humour. Redondo draws spaceships blessed with speed and grace, and uses his thumb-prints to create planet-sized explosions. Ezquerra's angles are extreme, things rip and tear; his is a dirty but thrilling future. Bellardinelli's aliens are all weird and funny and friendly and scary. There are British masters too: Bolland, McMahon and Smith; Gibbons, O'Neill and Davis. But they have surnames you might find at school or in a foot-ball team – they aren't exotic, they don't feel other and special.

I'm an actor of thirty-five, working on a film in Venice. I play a bishop's spy, on the trail of Casanova. We're dressed in wigs and the most extraordinary outfits, and work every day in *scuolas* and churches, walled with masterpieces by Titian, Tiepolo, Tintoretto. They are the motivational artwork in our offices. Venice is like wedding cake every day. The art is everywhere. I'm in the art, I'm part of the art. This too is special.

In between, I've done my growing up in a town as close to Calais as it is to London, and seen French children find our places exciting and exotic.

And since, I've worked in Würzburg, Barcelona, and Bucharest; Genoa, Brussels and Amsterdam. And each time I've worked on the mainland, I've felt the adventure of being in my own European story. I've had all the luck.

We may be the person at the left-hand edge of the picture, but I've always felt we're part of the group; the picture won't be complete without us.

WHAT EUROPE MEANS TO ME

Sue MacGregor

Europe! It was, for a child like me growing up in apartheid South Africa in the 1950s, a word loaded with meaning. Even in comparatively liberal Cape Town and its suburbs where we lived, there were uncompromising notices on park benches, on Post Office entrances, on access to almost all forms of entertainment, and even on sections on the bus which took me to school – 'Europeans Only' was the rule. In other words, if you weren't white, go elsewhere. The white Nationalist government that made these draconian laws weren't much interested in the geographical Europe from where their ancestors had set sail for the Cape. The majority of white Afrikaners looked on modern Europe with some scorn – it was the home of their fiercest critics, the sort of people who simply didn't understand how necessary it was to keep black and white apart.

But I was longing to escape all this after my school-days and return to the Europe from which my parents had emigrated some years after the War. I was despatched to Neuchâtel to attend a course on commercial French (and no it wasn't a finishing school). My stay there was pretty irrelevant to my subsequent career, but it left me with a lasting longing for lakes and mountains and snow in the winter.

I learned shorthand (not very useful) and typing (absolutely essential) back in Britain, where I made friends with fellow students and went with one of them on my first visit to Spain – a memorable early package tour to the Costa del Sol where a glass of wine on the beach cost sixpence and where the beaches were empty and stretched for miles.

I then found myself employed in London by the BBC on a temporary contract which somehow lasted for years and allowed for paid holidays. This meant I could ski, however tentatively at first, in the European mountains. There I made new friends, many of them German-speaking, in a small Austrian village to which we kept returning for decades. In the summer, Italy south of Naples was hugely attractive. Indeed, Ravello and Amalfi, before they became too crowded, were both heaven to visit. At the entrance to an old convent in Amalfi, now a charming hotel, a plaque announced that it had been a regular stopping-off point for Wagner. And thus, rather to my own astonishment, I found a taste for his music, after appreciating the brilliance of other European musical geniuses – Mozart, Schubert and Mendelssohn being early favourites.

And the food! It was in those days irresistibly better than anything I'd had in London. Now, of course, things are very different, but in those days the wonderfulness of Italian ice cream, the wicked delights of Austrian apfelstrudel and the profusion of delicious French wines were treats to be indulged in for two or three weeks every year. And so they remain.

I'm afraid my Love Letter to Europe is almost entirely hedonistic and possibly even trivial. Politics on both sides of the Channel are currently – how can I put it? – divisive, as we still seem far from a solution to the Brexit mess. But Europe – as an idea, as well as Europe as a destination – is well worth a love letter from across the Channel. Here's hoping the bureaucrats in Brussels can find somewhere to file it!

ITALIA MIA

Kevin Jackson

In July and August 1818, the poet and revolutionary Percy Shelley lived in a stone cottage just up the hill from the (then) remote country spa, Bagni di Lucca. He and his wife-to-be Mary spent their days having picnics, bathing in the chill streams, reading, playing chess and sometimes, of an evening, dancing at the local Casino. But Shelley also worked. Every morning, he would sit in the shade of a laurel tree and push on with his translation of Plato's *Symposium*, the subject of which is love. Surprisingly, since the *Symposium* is now one of the best-known works by Plato, this was only the second version of the text – the first was by the Cambridge scholar Thomas Taylor in 1792. Shelley's version is much better.

One reason why the *Symposium* had largely been shunned by classicists is its free and calm treatment of homosexual love. In retrospect, though, Shelley's text can also be seen as evidence of a much more respectable form of love – the English passion for Italy, which in its modern form really begins with Shelley and Byron and Keats and Walter Savage Landor (who in 1818 was living not far away, in Pisa). To be sure, the English had been travelling to Italy for many years – Wyatt on diplomatic business, Milton to encounter Galileo, young aristocrats being dragged around the ruins; there is even a folk tradition that Shakespeare travelled in the *bel paese*. (You only need to look at the plays set in Italy to see that this can't be true. Unless he was drunk all the time.) But the Italomania which so many of us continue to enjoy and endure begins with the English Romantics.

Bagni di Lucca was one of the places particularly dear to English writers. Robert and Elizabeth Barrett Browning used to spend their summers enjoying its cool breezes when their adopted home of Florence grew unbearably warm. There are traces of the English fondness for Bagni on all sides: in the English Library (a wonderful collection of books, it is said, stored uselessly as there is no librarian), and in the English Cemetery, where the once-famous novelist Ouida is buried.

And now, much to my surprise, I have yielded to the English Vice and have bought a modest house in Bagni, where my wife and I now spend brief holidays and hope to live permanently in years to come. I am quite content with the prospect of one day dying there, and perhaps having my ashes scattered near Ouida's resting place.

Opting to embrace Italy as my other country, my second home, feels like the culmination of a long-distance affair that began almost half a century ago. A few years before I ever visited the country, I was blown away by the Italian films shown on the BBC. Fellini! Visconti! Pasolini! De Sica! Antonioni! Rossellini! And it was at about this time that Bertolucci had his massive international hit with *Last Tango in Paris* . . . Whatever else the Italians might be, they were obviously filmmakers of genius.

At the age of eighteen, working as a raspberry-picker in Arbroath, I met my first Italian friend, Giorgio Presot: a dashing, slim-hipped, ultra-cool dude who looked like he should be a bass-player in a prog rock band and spoke embarrassingly good

English. Giorgio and I were both solemn boy outsiders, and we spoke for hours of T.E. Lawrence (a shared obsession), Hegel (new to me) and Gnosticism (Giorgio asked my friend Pete what his faith was; Pete said 'Agnostic', which Giorgio heard as 'A Gnostic'). Giorgio was my first friend from the Continent; he made me realise how much it enlarged the soul to have a friend who was at once so different and so much the same.

I was nineteen when I first travelled to Italy – hitch-hiked, in fact. Dawn was breaking as I lolled in the back of a hippy van, listening to Pink Floyd's *Ummagumma*, and saw Milan for the first time. The hippies dropped me off at the railway station, where I was disconcerted to be offered a thimble of jet fuel when I expected a big milky jug of instant coffee, and even more disconcerted to be given a handful of boiled sweets by way of change. (Loving Italy does not make you blind to its many, many maddening aspects.) When it was a respectable hour, I wandered over to the via Moscova where I would be staying for the next couple of weeks with my school pal Mark and his family. We mooched all around the city for the next few days and I admired everything from the elegant skyscraper that was home to the Pirelli company to the *Last Supper*, which in those innocent days was a free treat. We used the wonderfully cheap railways to explore the north of the country, especially Venice, where I had Mark take a picture of me posing outside Harry's Bar, and swore that I would go back there as a grown-up writer and drink a Martini. It took about three decades to make that dream a reality.

In my twenties I was mostly too poor to travel, but I did discover that Dante, whom I had first read in a bland translation, was not an insufferable bore as I had thought, but a dazzling genius when read, albeit slowly, in the original. My Virgil in this task was, once again, my friend Mark, who at this time (1983) was a schoolteacher, while I was working as a night security guard at the Arab-British Chamber of Commerce. Every Thursday evening, Mark would come to the empty offices and lead me line-by-line through the poem, glossing and commenting as we went. An unforgettable experience. Many years later, I produced a comic-book version of *Inferno* in collaboration with the brilliant cartoonist Hunt Emerson.

It was also in my twenties that I learned to love opera: Da Ponte's libretto for *The Marriage of Figaro* taught me my first Italian songs, unless you count *Bandliero Rosso* or *Volare*. From there it was only a short hop to Verdi and Puccini. And, guided partly by Cyril Connolly's *The Unquiet Grave*, I became fascinated by Italian writers, above all the magnificently melancholy Leopardi.

For a certain type of English person, a love of Italy is part of our cultural heritage – almost a component of our national DNA. Of course I also admire other nations and enjoy visiting their cities and their countryside, but Italy is my home-from-home, my other country. And though some of my compatriots have turned sour on Europe (a pox on them!), I stubbornly regard myself as European as well as English. Down with xenophobia! Hurrah for the Great Republic! And, above all, *Viva Italia!!*

COME LIVE WITH ME

THE BIG TRILL

Charles Nicholl

'Thou paradise of exiles, Italy!' The English Romantic poets are not great role-models when moving to Italy – for most of them it ended badly – but Shelley's rhapsodic line is hard to resist as a kind of slogan or booster for the move. His lovely synopsis of the Italian landscape – 'Mountains, seas and vineyards, and the towers / Of cities they encircle' – also plays in the mind as you pore over maps and plot reconnaissances.

Our little slice of paradise was an old farmhouse on a steep patch of south-facing land in the Apuan foothills of northern Tuscany. Had we bought it through an estate agent it would have been described as 'secluded' and 'in need of improvement'. A family of *contadini* had lived there for decades, originally as sharecroppers. They were ready to move – the old ones worn out and the young ones unenthused by a life of subsistence toil. Buying the house was predictably slow and tortuous, but eventually we were there at the local notary's office, carrying a sports bag bulging with millions of lire, and the contract was signed. Even then there were further delays – some bureaucratic, some personal – before we were finally jolting up the track in a plume of dust, to 'take possession'.

The place was literally buzzing. The house had been empty for several hot summer months – empty, that is, of humans – and in their absence squatters of all shapes and sizes had swiftly moved in. There were hornets nesting in the chimney, which resonated with a deep bass hum. There were bats in the rafters, a toad or two in a damp corner of the *cantina*, and lizards everywhere. And of course, this being paradise, there were serpents. My first snake encounter was a couple of days later, when I pushed aside an old car-tyre and found that its curiously patterned inner tube was a metre-long yellow-green coluber, known locally as a *frustone* or 'big whip'. This snake is allegedy 'harmless', which broadly means it can bite you but not poison you.

Over the next few months our sightings would include buzzards, kites, bee-eaters and hoopoes; wild boar, foxes, roe deer, porcupines, martens and the charming squirrel-tailed dormouse called a *ghiro*.

We lived in Italy for fifteen years and still go back there as often as we can. We have been blessed with our share of *dolce vita* moments and with many fine friendships, but I will always remember that first evening in the wilds, looking out over our demesne of rampant Mediterranean scrub, drinking in the sounds and smells along with some glasses of cheap *vino frizzante* 'with beaded bubbles winking at the brim'. As the light fades, the cicadas tune up for their nightly performance: the big trill. It echoes all down the hillside and along the valley, a long, lulling overture so monotonous you can almost believe this moment will never end.

THE VIEW AT SUNSET

Chris Cleave

British people praising Europe's merits can often sound like the ritual film segment in which Roger Moore's James Bond shows off to Bernard Lee's spy chief, M.

'What do you know about the Brèche des Drus, 007?'

'The jagged ridge that joins the Petit Dru and the Grand Dru, sir, high above the Chamonix valley. More serious than anything we've got.'

'I see you've done your homework, Bond – now what about Maurice Merleau-Ponty?'

'Gallic phenomenologist, sir – they say he runs rings around our philosophers.'

I can't really express that suave kind of admiration for Europe, because I'm not 007 material. In the Bond film of life, I'm Francisco Scaramanga's diminutive henchman, Nick Nack: I'm conflicted, I'm a little bit French, and if I get too annoying you can easily stuff me into a wicker basket and hoist me up the mast of a ship – which is what Bond does at the end of *The Man with the Golden Gun*. Nick Nack is no more than a curiosity and an irritation in that quintessentially British movie, but mighty indeed are those viewers who don't feel some pang of recognition in his poignant line, 'I may be small, but I never forget.'

European readers of this anthology will have known for a while that this is an era in which we British are quick to forget facts and to put our stock in rhetoric instead. As a nation we recently took part in a war on 'terror', and this time we are committed to sacrifice for the sake of 'sovereignty'.

When I was twenty-eight, long before the current hostilities were declared, I married a European. In my defence, I was an EU citizen myself at the time – my people having voted by a huge majority for that to be so. And for the record, I didn't marry Clémence because I had the hots for European constitutional ratification. I married her because she's vivacious, beautiful and kind, and because the idea of becoming Mrs Nick Nack didn't bother her as much as it probably should have. Reflecting on it now, I have no idea why she married me. Britannia was cool at the time, and some of the glamour may have attached to my person. The Union Flag was something that people in Milan and Copenhagen had on their lounge cushions and coffee cups. I believe it was never part of the EU's founding remit to help British citizens date people who were out of their league, but in my case it was a welcome epiphenomenon.

Clémence and I met at work, in London. French people used to flock in huge numbers to study and work in our capital, and if you want to know why then you'd better ask them quickly, because that particular train is leaving the station. Clémence arrived in London Waterloo on the first Eurostar on a Friday morning – with thirty-three euros in her bank account and Plastic Bertrand's 'Ça Plane Pour Moi' on her headphones – and she had a job by Monday lunchtime. Nineteen years and three vivacious, beautiful and kind Anglo-French children later, I still think of my wife as the perfect embodiment of freedom of movement.

Clémence does precise extremely of the grammar now, although initially not excellent was her speaking of the English. These days she talks like a British native and she also swears like one. The effect is brilliant and terrifying because in the *Top Trumps* of profanity, my wife has no idea of the relative killing power of the various English swear-words. She is enduringly popular at the school gate for once having used our infamous C-word to describe a teacher whom she liked a lot but who was setting our children slightly too much homework. Another charming thing about living with an enemy of the people is that she mishears our national idioms, and the effect is so endearing that I don't always rush to correct her. Clém, if you're reading this: I'm sorry – it's 'In this day and age', not 'In this dying age'. Even we Brits aren't quite that morbid.

If I've made my wife sound like a comic turn, she isn't. She's a trained economist who's worked for lastminute.com, the National Archives and the Cabinet Office. (For the benefit of European readers I should explain that these are three iconic British institutions that respectively represent entrepreneurship, our collective national memory, and any particularly difficult dossier that you would have to file under 'other'.) Right now, having retrained as a clinical nutritionist, my wife is helping young people to recover from eating disorders. She still can't bullseye the pronunciation of the words *crisps*, *Gloucestershire* or *squirrels*, and yet there are young British people who are in clinical recovery today solely because Clémence didn't need a corporate job offer or a minimum bank balance when she came to the UK in the summer of 1999.

Following the Brexit vote, my wife and I took each other's citizenship. We did it as a renewal of our vows: as an affirmation that we didn't want to lose the link with the other and with the other's culture. And maybe in the backs of our minds we also did it as a safety precaution – just in case England's current political adventure turned out to be the age of a new golden dawn, rather than the dawn of a new golden age.

For Clémence, citizenship meant having to prove decades of financial self-sufficiency. She also had to learn which Brits won which medals in the 1992 Olympics, in order to pass the *Life in the UK* test. In the multiple-choice history section of that test it was necessary to check any boxes indicating that Britain had stood alone against evil during the Second World War. If a free-text response had been available instead, my wife could have mentioned that during the occupation, her family hid foreign Jews in their house just outside Paris, and that when suspicious neighbours commented on their protégés' thick accents, they simply bluffed that their guests were from Brittany. Six decades later, those Holocaust survivors' grandchildren came to our wedding and we all danced to DJs who happened to be nationals of the former Axis powers.

For me, citizenship meant a language test and an interview with the French vice-consul in which she asked me to explain what I intended to contribute to French cultural life. Imagine a British *Plastic Bertrand*, I said – only smaller, more anxious, and willing to operate from a little wicker basket hoisted up the mast of some jointly operated Anglo-French aircraft carrier. I'm paraphrasing of course, but it turned out that France did have a vacancy in roughly that role, and so she kindly approved my application.

The process of becoming a French citizen increased my admiration for France even as it enhanced my appreciation of being

British. My wife is from a sprawling Franco-Italian family with cousins to visit all over Europe, and something I've loved about living with her is that over two decades I've learned and integrated many different European perspectives, without compromising my native Britishness. Indeed, the contrasts have shown me what being British means, and how important a quality Britishness is to communicate – even to undeserving foreigners like you. This integrationist perspective once made me a cultural ambassador for the UK. How suddenly it now makes me a pariah.

At the moment of writing, English people who literally wear top hats in their free time are using a bought-off media to boost the view that it's elitist to hope for continued cooperation with our European allies. If our current English masters continue with their project of disinformation and division, they'll soon have succeeded in their goal of turning our European allies into our enemies. Memory is short, and people like me might soon be seen as dinosaurs, or even as traitors – but this is certainly the first time Nick Nack has been accused of representing an elite.

In truth I've always felt terrified, under-skilled and under-protected – which I think makes me a very normal British person. Like most people on our islands, I'm scared of the problems we've generated all on our own: poverty, lawlessness and violence. I think it's pretty ordinary of me to wonder why we will always bail out the bankers but never the nurses or the teachers. And on a personal level – also like anyone, I think – I wish I were younger and smarter. As a middle-aged writer I've chosen a beautiful and stupid vocation where I'm inevitably at the bottom of the corporate food chain, and I don't blame anyone for that but myself. I get through the day by nervously projecting self-confidence while blasting pop music through my headphones to block out the money worries.

Is this really how being 'elite' feels? I'm the diminutive state-educated offspring of an ordinary family of modest means. All our clothes were second-hand or sewn by my mum, but that didn't feel particularly wrong: it was the seventies and eighties, and I don't remember anyone having money. My brother and I worried about the ordinary things: hairstyles and nuclear war. Our aunt was an anti-nuclear protestor camping outside an American airbase called Greenham Common, and our favourite thing was roller discos. Our closest Tube station was Amersham, which is as far out as you can go on the Metropolitan Line without coming up in the Atlantic.

An area where I do acknowledge my privilege is that nobody racially abused or sexually harassed me. No one bullied me either, despite my home-sewn clothes, my shyness, and my actual roller skates. As I grew older I did some really senseless things, but people gave me second chances.

Brexit has made me feel smaller, shyer and less stable on my skates, but it has also shown me how much I love the UK and how grateful I am for what it's given me. I don't feel the rancour I'm supposed to be feeling. Instead I feel genuine kinship with people, equally including the ones who voted the opposite way from me. I've learned through years of engagement that my love for Europe is not incompatible with my love for the UK. On the contrary, I've understood that the qualities we admire can only be those we have learned to value – and so when a British person writes of their love for Europe, of course what they're really expressing is the love of Britain: that helpless first love, in the crucible of which all subsequent desires are formed.

So if I admit that in fact my heart really does catch irresistibly on the bladed ridgelines of the Alps, then that's only because my heart first raced on the ridges of Striding Edge and Tryfan where my dad took me scrambling. If I shy from conviction and escape instead into the humbler world of French phenomenology, then it's because Turner taught me how to receive ambiguity, how to navigate evanescence, how to see in an uncertain light. And if I write – on balance, despite the inevitable compromises of cooperation, despite the regrettable choice of the *Ode to Joy* rather than the Queen/Bowie collaboration 'Under Pressure' for the anthem – if I write that I'm nonetheless attracted to a European project that defends the rights of its citizens against the tyranny of top-hatted capital, then this must be seen as the considered view of a democrat, steeped from the cradle in the love of British ideas. I can express such a view only because Magna Carta, William Wilberforce and Annie Besant taught me that the most serious purpose of democracy is to defend us from stockpiled wealth, which is quite capable of defending itself.

Through engagement with Europe I've learned that Britishness is a clement thing, wonderful to have been born into, extraordinarily easy to love. Its climate is mild, its mountains modest, its philosophers possessed of a pragmatism that is readable and unflashy. At the drop of a hat, without waiting for the state to give us impetus or permission, our people form benevolent organisations to help each other out: you can witness our national character in Parkrun, or the Royal National Lifeboat Institution, or the Terrence Higgins Trust. And when we British find each other demoralised, we often make use of a quietly absurd humour that lifts the spirits without requiring any scapegoat. The reason we don't always have to raise a rabble is that we know how to raise an eyebrow.

So I hope I have explained to you how Nick Nack feels in the sunset at the end of the movie, now that Bond has hoisted him up the mast in his tiny wicker cage. Nick Nack has one eyebrow raised and a sad half-smile as he watches the coastline receding. My heart is full of love and I'm not moaning, or fomenting, or otherwise thwarting the will of the people. It's just that if anyone asks me what the view is like from my lookout, I can only tell them the truth: that I can see the Europe I love quite well from up here, but it's getting further away.

ONE OF US

Sophie Sabbage

My husband proposed to me in a restaurant next to the famous Ponte Vecchio in Florence. It was New Year's Eve. The air was icy, but the city was teeming with tourists and, during the day, gleamed burnished gold in the winter sunlight. We had only been dating for three months, but the exuberant palaces, museums and masterpieces seemed to mirror the wonderment we were feeling for each other. It wasn't romantic as much as authentic. True beauty. True renaissance. True love.

John hadn't planned to propose, I learned later. It just burst out of him that evening, partly induced by our surroundings. As we stood on the restaurant balcony after dinner, poised for the year to turn and our lives to merge, crowds were forming on both banks of the River Arno. Suddenly, everyone on our side started counting down to midnight in sonorous Italian: '10, 9, 8, 7, 6, 5, 4, 3, 2, 1. *Felice Anno Nuovo*!' A few seconds later, everyone on the other side of the river repeated the countdown and a chorus of laughter erupted with the exploding fireworks. It reminded me of that tacky but tickling tourist T-shirt, 'Heaven is where the cooks are French, the lovers are Italian, the police are British, and everything is organised by the Germans. Hell is where the cooks are German, the lovers are British, the police are French, and everything is organised by the Italians.'

My heart breaks a little as I write that. There *is* something heavenly about the collective cultural aptitudes of a dazzling civilisation that has evolved over millennia; about driving freely through France, Spain and Portugal, as we did on our honeymoon, relishing their distinct and nuanced rhythms; about German bratwursts, French cheese, Spanish tapas, Greek salads, Italian arancini; about the warp and weft of artistic European movements down the ages; about the peace I've experienced on this continent my entire life. I am a very proud European.

I recently gave a TEDx talk in a largely pro-Brexit corner of England. The hosts opened the event by asking where we were all from, starting with local towns in the area, extending out to the rest of the UK and ultimately asking if anyone was from Europe.

'We all are!' shouted a man sitting near the front of the theatre, at which the thousand-strong audience roared with laughter and cheered in unison. It simultaneously lifted my spirits and augmented the grief I was to speak about that day.

For thirty years, I have helped thousands of individuals and dozens of leading businesses to shift the self-deceiving, inaccurate mindsets that limit their evolution. In recent years, as an author and patient activist living with terminal cancer, I've also been helping fellow patients distinguish between perception and reality, to make decisions about their treatment based on what is so rather than what is feared or denied. Then we can live and even die peacefully, knowing we made our very best choices along the way.

Would that we could apply these principles to our relationship with the EU, where the perceived invasion of detrimental foreign influences on British life has obscured the actual invasion of resentful nostalgia seeking to resurrect bygone days of bowler hats, British Leyland, mandatory Sunday roasts and Mighty Blighty. This is not the whole story, but it is the part we're not attending to, along with some simple and long borne-out wisdoms: that interdependence is more transformative than independence; that the end of aloneness is the felt experience of all-one-ness; that by raising others up we raise up ourselves.

Two years after our wedding, John and I drove across Europe again, this time to Umbria with a hard-won embryo in my womb. I didn't know I was pregnant until we reached the villa, which we had rented for two months – either to grieve the failure of this last attempt for a baby or to put my body into deep rest during the first trimester. Once again, I was in Italy for this ecstatic moment: seeing two pink lines on the pregnancy test while John wrapped his arms around my incredulity and said, 'Yes, babe. There really are two lines.'

A few days later I started to bleed. We were hundreds of miles away from my obstetrician. Neither of us spoke Italian. Fear entered. Regret that we had come. Self-accusations of stupidity and recklessness. Longing for lush green fields instead of sunburnt hills. Homesickness. Desperation. Prayers.

Somehow John got me to the nearest hospital, armed with the Italian words for 'pregnant' and 'blood', where an obstetrician of small stature and kind eyes did an ultrasound of my belly. He spoke almost no English and our Italian was worse, but we fumbled our way into a shared understanding, occasionally using Google to translate.

'Today baby ok,' he eventually told us. 'Tomorrow, don't know. Come back.'

The next day, he said it again. 'Today, baby ok. Tomorrow, don't know. Come back.'

And this was how it rolled, our increasing gratitude for his care matched only by increasing anxiety about the final bill even as the gaps between visits were extended by 'Next week, don't know. Come back.'

A few days before we were due to make the long drive home, we saw our dedicated Italian obstetrician for the last time. First, he took my hand after the ultrasound and said, 'Send me a photo.' I threw my arms around him. Second, John presented our EU health card and asked, '*Quanto costa?*'

'*No, niente. Sei uno di noi,*' replied the stranger who had saved my baby in a foreign land. 'No. Nothing. You are one of us.'

Six months later another European, by the name of Gabriella (a very popular name in Italy), was born. Her uncertain arrival had been ensured by an Umbrian obstetrician who treated us like compatriots, our membership of a valuable union and by her second name – Grace.

MOONSTONES ON THE CAMPIDOGLIO

Lindsey Davis

I am a European. Like many British people and quite a few of our politicians, I have a political migrant from Europe among my ancestors. Almost by chance I ended up writing about ancient Rome.

For over thirty years I have learned about Rome, visited Rome, and come to love the city and its people, then and now. My work has made me many friends in other European countries.

In 2009, for the biennial of Vespasian, 'my' Emperor, the city of Rome inaugurated the Premio Colosseo, a prize which was awarded to the famous film director, Franco Zeffirelli. The next year, they awarded the prize to me. What I said to them in thanks was my love letter not only to Rome but also to Europe; it was what I felt then, and still applies now.

At short notice – this was Italy – I found myself invited to 'a gala evening on the Campidoglio, with many guests'. It seemed to be true, for there was a press notice:

> Lindsey Davis, the historical novelist, has been invited by the Mayor of Rome to a Gala Evening on 5 November at the prestigious Terrazza Caffarelli, where she will be awarded the Premio Colosseo. The special prize, an original silver sculpture of the Colosseum by Ferdinando Codognotto, will be

given each year to individuals who have enhanced the image of Rome through their work in culture, art, journalism, tourism, entertainment, business or scientific research.

Amazement. One thing I thought was how unlikely it would be for any Mayor to give a prize to a foreigner for enhancing London's image – especially since our Mayor at the time was the self-absorbed Boris Johnson . . .

Ten days of shopping passed in a blur of anxiety. I ended up with expensive garments, accessorised with a necklace by a designer who had once made a head-dress for Kylie Minogue. I also had very dangling moonstone earrings, a Wilkie Collins tribute that was probably lost on everyone. With this gear in carry-on luggage, I set off.

I deduced that my Premio Colosseo was perhaps not entirely for fine writing, but a thank-you for bringing Falco readers to Rome on holiday. My fellow guests included foreign tour operators who had spent much time being shown half-built hotels and an unfinished aquarium. On the night, we were taken by coach to the gala with a police escort, accompanied by sirens. That was *very* exciting. We then discovered that Michelangelo did not design the Campigdolio steps for evening shoes.

The Deputy Mayor handed me my prize. I had met him before, so I greeted him and thanked him with warm continental cheek-kissing. He took it well.

A glamorous female presenter in a long scarlet gown was then supposed to ask me questions. At her first weary murmur of 'So what made you write about Rome? . . .' I flipped. I grabbed her microphone. I had brought a speech. I had spent three days creating it. My Italian publicist had advised 'just say nice things'

– and although he's a Milanese Calvinist, when he read my speech in advance it made him cry.

I was going to say my piece. If this was a gala evening, I would make it zing. They expected an elderly English lady in the dowdy be-cardiganed mould, but I had on a necklace by a designer who kitted out Kylie. So, I deliberately set out to smooch Europe on European terms: I would be more passionately tear-jerking than the European Song Contest.

Here are some extracts. 31 October 2019 seems a moment for a reprise:

First, I apologise for not speaking in Italian. The British are still barbarians, I'm afraid, even though the Roman historian Tacitus described attempts to civilise us and said, 'Instead of loathing the Latin language they became eager to speak it.' Many of us still know more of Latin than modern languages, and indeed the current Mayor of London, where I live, often gives speeches in Latin. It causes consternation. But it shows the respect we have for your heritage, a respect that deeply colours my work.

For twenty years it has been my privilege to write about Rome. To me, neither your city nor the civilisation it produced really needs any enhancement, but I am delighted to have played my part in bringing Rome to the notice of readers around the world.

The one regret I have tonight is that my partner Richard, who died two years ago, can't be here. From the moment we first came, when I had just begun writing, Rome was 'our' city. We spent very many happy hours in your wonderful museums and archaeological sites, basking in your climate, enjoying your cuisine. We also loved just to wander, with no particular aim and hardly looking at the map, just observing places and people and absorbing the atmosphere. We came every year. My love for your city is intricately bound up with the love we had for each other. It has always affected the way I present Rome in my books. Rome is a city of love and I think you will appreciate that.

To write about a great city and then to be recognised by that city for what you have done must be the highest achievement for an author. I am overwhelmed that you have chosen to give me the Premio Colosseo. This is an extraordinary honour, which I accept with much emotion, and I thank you very much indeed.

It made me cry (and I was sober). Ladies sobbed, gents looked bemused. The Deputy Mayor let me kiss him again.

The velvet-lined box with the original silver sculpture was too big for my hand luggage. I brought the prize home wrapped in a fluffy sock.

That was a warm and wonderful evening. I was a European that night and, dammit, I always will be. Remembering, this is my love letter to Europe.

A FRENCH AFFAIR

Patricia Atkinson

Without knowing it, as a child I was already a bit of a European. I lived in Germany and Malta before my family returned to Britain. For the last thirty years or so, I have lived in south-west France as a winemaker.

I moved to France all those years ago attracted by the idyll of its culture and lifestyle, so European and so utterly unlike ours. After protracted dealings we bought a small house with a few hectares of vines and moved in.

I remember that first evening as if it were yesterday. It was hot and balmy, the heady scent of the privet hedge adding to the exotic ambience of the courtyard in which we were sitting, a chorus of cicadas providing a loud and hypnotic backdrop. A glass of cold rosé was in my hand. Balanced on the low make-shift table next to us was a plateful of those wonderful French crudités – tiny delicacies of meats and vegetables in unusual sauces and flavoured with herbs and spices. In those days we had nothing like that in Britain.

Basking in the euphoria of the evening and intoxicated by the wine, the perfume of the privet and the beauty of the sunset, I remember thinking how privileged the French were to have all this and how privileged I was to be part of it.

My house sits on the ridge of a low rolling hillside. It's

peaceful and unspoilt, surrounded by vines, their sinuous curves following the contours of the landscape – carpets of lush green. To the north the land drops steeply away to the valley of the Dordogne, its fields and vines creating a tapestry of yellow and green, its perimeters studded by historical monuments. Fruit trees and vines have been cultivated here for hundreds of years, agriculture being an essential part of this region. Forests of oaks, walnuts, and chestnuts abound. Tobacco, maize and cereal crops are grown and, of course, wine is made here.

When I arrived, I'm ashamed to say I didn't speak French and knew nothing about vines, wine or winemaking. Looking back on it, what was I thinking? How could I have considered moving here with no real idea of what I was doing? To be fair, I wasn't planning to be the one making wine at all – it just turned out that way. And once I started, it was immediate, intense and insane, learning to speak French, drive tractors and make wine simultaneously. Which just goes to show that when needs must . . .

Now, of course, I can speak French and drive tractors and make wine too. But none of that could have been achieved without the French. Their spontaneous generosity and acts of kindness are just too numerous to mention – a few will suffice.

Like the time the sprayer fell off the back of the tractor as I was driving up and down the rows of vines. I'd been spraying for hours, for most of the day, dulled into a desultory dream-like state by the rhythmic sound of the motor. I was almost done and feeling relieved to have provided the necessary protection to the vines before the thunderstorm forecast for that evening. In the distance I could hear other tractors doing the same thing.

Without warning, the heavy sprayer attached behind and sitting high above the tractor fell off. It hit the ground with an earth-shattering crash and the tractor reared up dangerously in response. The motor of the sprayer emitted a high-pitched, ear-piercing whine while spraying its contents in the sky, on the feet of the vines and over me. The front wheels of the tractor were no longer on the ground. How I didn't kill myself that day I don't know.

My nearest neighbour, Gilles, was spraying his vines and heard it – indeed the whole village heard it. He bounded over the fields and arrived at the same time as my friend, Michel, the local council worker who was also working in the area. Between them, while being sprayed violently by the blue copper sulphate cascading out, they somehow switched off the tractor and the motor of the sprayer with it.

The silence after the roar of the tractor and the sprayer was eerie and still. A wasp in search of a sugary grape buzzed lazily by as we looked down at the damage, caked blue copper sulphate covering our skin and clothes. The nozzles of the sprayer were piled on the ground.

With various tools, Gilles and Michel succeeded in reattaching the nozzles, then reattaching the spraying machine to the back of the tractor. I shakily remounted it and cautiously sprayed the last two rows of vines.

In fact, Gilles and Michel were often my saviours, as when I broke my leg the following year just as the spraying season began. They simply sprayed my vines for me. They had their own vines to manage and I know it must have cost them greatly in time, if nothing else. Or when they helped me to prune, hour after hour in the vines, and to attach the lats to the wires when we had a race against time.

I had similar help in the wine cellar from my oenologist and from fellow winemakers. Many of them came to pick at my vineyard during the harvest when they weren't picking at their own. One of my neighbours gave me an entire plot of grapes as he had reached the legal quota for his harvest. Not only did he give me the grapes but he helped pick them too.

Such generosity of spirit, such acceptance, such consideration and such genuine kindness is inspiring. I hope, but am not sure, I would have had that in Britain, and I wonder if a Frenchman arriving in England not speaking the language and attempting to produce something British people had the monopoly on would have been treated as gently and humanely as I was? This, for me, is the essence of Europe. Europe's about people, it's about heritage and inclusion and peace.

It changed my life for the better and has made me richer in every way. And whether or not British people think so, Europe as a whole has changed and enriched their lives too – one only has to think back to how Britain was before we joined.

I'm so sad at the prospect of no longer being part of this wonderful community which is so much more diverse and more open than we have become in Britain. We will miss it when we no longer have it, that's for sure. I love being part of a family of twenty-seven countries, I love benefitting from its unity, from its thousands of years of shared history with its rich cultural heritage. I can't imagine why any of us in Britain should be reluctant to remain a part of it.

LUCKIER THAN SOME

Marcus Sedgwick

Maybe I was luckier than some – I didn't even have to go to Europe to fall in love with it; it came to me, as a young child.

My father ran a group of English as a Foreign Language schools in Kent in the seventies and eighties. My mother worked there too, finding homes for the foreign students in the local area, and so as young boys my brother and I would often spend evenings and holidays hanging around one or other of the centres, mixing with young people from not just Europe, but all over the world.

I remember impressions of various students: presents of traditional dolls from Greece; cool French students who came for lunch at our house one summer; generous Germans offering me wine at inappropriate ages. All of them were friendly, all of them so interesting – I saw hints and glimpses of the Europe I would later come to love during an exchange holiday to Germany and Austria, a trip to Amsterdam, holidays in France as a young adult, and later, my greatest love of all, Sweden.

I also remember back to the stories my mother told me; about the sometimes funny things that would occur between students and their host families; little misunderstandings of culture here and there, but never any real problems, never any animosity. From time to time she'd report how an Italian student, for example, had encouraged the reluctant husband in a host family to try pasta for the first time, with happy results.

All I saw was good. There was no fear of the other; there was a gentle curiosity and a wonderful integration of cultures. I wouldn't have been able to articulate this then, but looking back it's clear that this is the direction I thought we were heading in – the joy of respect and interest in different lands and people; the simultaneous unity of existing as part of one larger family. Beethoven's *Ninth* as the soundtrack to whatever peeks of Europe I saw on the television, long before I ever went there; be it *Jeux Sans Frontières* or *Eurovision* or a late-night broadcast of a European Cup game. I loved it all.

Today, I live in France. We have been made utterly welcome by our French neighbours, who, if the subject arises, can only scratch their heads in utter bemusement at why we would want to leave this union. I try to explain, but in order to really understand, you have to be British. Or rather, not British, but a certain English sort – that peculiar, insular, self-aggrandising mentality that cannot see past the White Cliffs of Kent. I have never understood that, but then perhaps I was lucky; I lived on the doorstep of mainland Europe. And it came to see me.

THE GEORGE SANDERS LONG WALK

Roger Lewis

One day I'll make a pilgrimage to the Hotel Rey Don Jaime in Castelldefels, ten miles south of Barcelona, where George Sanders committed suicide. ('Dear World,' he characteristically wrote in his over-egged note for the police, 'I am leaving because I am bored . . . I am leaving you with your worries in this sweet cesspool . . .') Meanwhile, there's always the Hotel Excelsior, in Naples, where Sanders, and Ingrid Bergman, made *Journey to Italy*, in 1954. 'What noisy people,' says Sanders' Alexander Joyce of the Italians, with amused irritation, or irritated amusement. 'I've never seen noise and boredom go so well together.'

If in England we have the antic perkiness of Arthur Askey, George Formby or Norman Wisdom; or at the other extreme the pinched depressiveness of Tony Hancock and Peter Cook (whose philosophy at the finish was boiled down to 'Why bother?') – with George Sanders there is a different quality of weariness, which was never wearisome, and which brought with it an impression of brittle sophistication, aristocratic despair, an expansiveness, which is European rather than provincial. Bitter lemons, as it were, rather than the English smell of burnt knicker elastic, mouldy carpets and malt vinegar. Sanders would have been good, it now occurs to me, in the Burt Lancaster role as the ancient and noble Sicilian prince, Don Fabrizio Corbera, in

The Leopard. (Instead of which he was the purring voice of Shere Khan, the tiger, in Disney's *Jungle Book*.)

In *Journey to Italy* we have two big Hollywood stars, dressed immaculately, if inappropriately. Sanders is in a succession of heavy tweed overcoats, lounge suits, jackets and ties. Bergman is wrapped in leopard skins and furs – in the Neapolitan sunshine. Yet there is never a bead of perspiration, as the characters are surrounded by Roberto Rossellini's documentary Italian realism – the shabby streets and tourist sites, the careworn, black-clad populace (everyone in mourning clothes), the location-work in hotel lobbies and catacombs.

Sanders and Bergman (whom Rossellini had married controversially in 1950) remain in legendary guise – him with his ducal, detached air, her with those dark eyes, inquisitive and wary, which made her so expert at portraying victims and missionaries. 'Where are we?' Sanders asks, in the opening line of the film. 'Oh, I don't know exactly,' Bergman replies. They are mythical beasts, dropped from Olympus. She is Katharine Joyce, the surname a clue – as throughout the film she pines for a lost, early love, an unpublished poet. 'He was slender, blond, tall, so delicate and romantic,' she reminisces – as Greta Conroy reminisces, in *The Dead*.

As regards the present plot, the Joyces are in Naples to see about selling some property they have inherited from an Uncle Homer. They squabble, exchange sarcastic remarks, pose stiffly before local landmarks, the Museum of Archaeology, with its miles of marble statuary, the Cave of the Cumaean Sibyl, and their marriage is turning brown, shrivelling and dying as we watch. 'At home everything seemed so perfect,' says Bergman, 'but now that we're away, alone—' 'Yes,' cuts in Sanders, 'it's a strange discovery to make.'

They are a wealthy, empty couple, with nothing in common, except the Bentley – a 1950 Bentley Mark VI drop-head coupe. 'We English aren't allowed to enjoy long stays abroad,' Bergman says – abroad, as it were, undoes us, exposes us: emotionally, physically – and as Bergman was Swedish and Sanders was born in St Petersburg, there's a joke there on lots of layers. Sanders, nevertheless, goes off on his own for a few days to Capri and Ischia, classical home of decadent emperors and exiles like William Walton, Truman Capote and W.H. Auden. Bergman hires a guide and inspects the bubbling sulphur pools at Vesuvius. The pair of them are reunited at Pompeii, and the sight in the ruins of a petrified man and woman, entwined for eternity, is heavily symbolic. Time, to quote a well-known poem, has transfigured them into untruth.

Dependent, as *Journey to Italy* is, on the grainy actuality of the city and adjacent hotspots, it's interesting that the final scene, where the Joyces are 'reconciled' during a religious procession, the Feast of San Gennaro, is the very one where everyone, extras included, looks like they are on a sound stage. It's as if Sanders and Bergman, an actor and an actress after all, radiating glamour and fame, can at last indulge in some (sentimental) acting, repeating lines from a script, and the scene is literally incredible, thoroughly let's pretend: 'Tell me that you love me! Tell me! I want to hear you say it!' – 'Well, if I do, will you promise not to take advantage of me?'

Sanders in real life was married lots of times, quite often to Zsa Zsa or Magda Gabor, and always lonely, which he equated with independence and freedom. He cultivated the sort of aloof loneliness that women liked, which they are always drawn to and wish to assuage. But he was never to be assuaged – anyone who came close might take advantage of him, see – and he was the cinema's great poet of dry cynicism, which became part of his style; the laureate of the stale, the acrid. He was an incomparable ironist, too. He once said the only thing he could remember about Zsa Zsa was that he could never talk to her because she was always under the hair dryer.

The silky baritone delivery was parodied by Peter Sellers' Hercules Grytpype-Thynne in *The Goon Show*, and even though Sanders, in later years, ended up supporting comedians (with Sellers in *A Shot in the Dark*, Hancock in *The Rebel*, Charlie Drake [Christ!] in *The Cracksman*), he was never tarnished by the association. Sanders had more depth, more seriousness, for example, than Dennis Price (though they are similar: superciliousness, fastidiousness); more masculinity, one could say, which always gave a clip and trot to the languor.

Three years prior to *Journey to Italy* he'd won the Oscar for Addison de Witt, in *All About Eve*. But I prefer Sanders here, where there is absolutely no camp, and where there is perhaps actual pain, which was connected to his majestic, cosmic self-contempt. 'I have no friends,' he'd frequently boast to interviewers, in the two decades remaining to him. 'No relations, no family. Everyone is dead. Now I am going to die too . . . I have no interests. I have no plans. I don't know where society is going and I don't care. I'm just happy I won't be around to see it.'

Nor was he, after his barbiturate-crammed body was found by the hotel manager, Juan Carbonell, on 25 April 1972. In *The Sopranos*, when Tony first consults Dr Melfi, he refers to his fear about making or replicating what he calls 'the George Sanders long walk here'. Later in the series, when the gangsters make their own journey to Italy, they stay at the Hotel Excelsior,

Naples. I mention this not to make anything of it, but I, too, have a house in the raw and remote Molise, a two-hour drive from the Aeroporto Internazionale di Napoli. Here I gather strength. 'We English aren't allowed long stays abroad' – but I am Welsh, and I don't mind being undone, being exposed psychologically. It's what being an artist means.

OPENING THE DOOR
A LITTLE WIDER

Nick Hayes, *Jazz club, Graz, Austria.*

WHERE THE ACTION WAS

Prue Leith

I was brought up in post-World War Two South Africa and we lived a very comfortable white, privileged life. But by the time I got to university in Cape Town, I was convinced that my country was a backwater. Everything, but everything, was happening 'overseas'.

My desire was unfocused. I just wanted to go where the action was. What action? I'd no idea. Where? Not a clue. If the opportunity had come to go to any big city anywhere at all, I'd have grabbed it.

I managed to persuade my long-suffering father that I needed to go to France to learn French from real French people. So it was that I found myself in Paris, enrolled first at the Alliance Française language school, and then at the Sorbonne.

Paris wasn't just a culture shock – it was life changing. Up till then the idea of being a cook had never crossed my mind. At home we'd had a great Zulu cook called Charlie, but no one suggested I learn at his apron strings. And my mother couldn't boil an egg. Besides, it was considered vulgar to talk of food, as it was of money, sex or God. Lord knows what we did talk about.

But in Paris everyone talked about food all the time. The family for which I was au pair talked of little else. Everyone wanted to know what was for lunch and there was much discussion at dinner parties about the best restaurants, where the beef was raised, about regional cheeses.

Madame insisted on the best; we'd go to three bakeries each morning, one for the croissants, one for the baguettes, one for the patisserie. When I stupidly asked why, she shrugged, eyes to heaven. 'You English,' (for her South African meant English) 'you know nothing about food.'

I'll never forget my first children's supper with her. There was a six-month-old baby and a toddler and, at 5pm, they ate exactly what we'd eat later. No Heinz jars or frozen fish fingers. But two tiny steaks, seared on both sides, rare in the middle. A *salade de laitue* turned in homemade dressing, new potatoes tossed in butter with chives, and a piece of baguette on the side. Both dished up on small plates. The toddler sat in her highchair and Maman cut up her dinner and sat beside her. I whizzed the baby's plateful in a liquidiser and fed her on my lap. We sat down, knees under, and talked to them as they ate.

I sometimes think that was my food lesson for life: simple recipe, fresh ingredients, cooked at the last minute from scratch, sit down and talk. That's what food is for.

But the culture shock wasn't confined to food. I thought Paris would be full of the sort of French people I'd read about in books. What surprised me was how many of those thronging the left bank were people of colour. In apartheid South Africa, where black children were only educated for free until the age of ten, where jobs as basic as lift operator or bricklayer were reserved for whites, where black people needed a pass to come into town and then only to work in menial subservient jobs, I had never met a black person as an equal. It did not, to my later shame, seem wrong to me that venerable old men would step off the pavement to let a bunch of giggling white schoolgirls past, or that our nanny had to sit in the back of the bus while we children went to the front.

Yet, as a young adult, I considered myself liberal-minded. I'd protested in Cape Town at the ban on black students, chanting for equality for all South Africans.

But I was unprepared for the reality of equality. I was now sitting next to Indian, Arab, and African students at lectures, in cafes and restaurants. Initially I found it disconcerting. To find myself in the *Boul' Mich'* flirted with and whistled at by Moroccans was at first frightening and then exciting. But soon I was eating couscous at street stalls with Algerian students and talking about Rimbaud and Verlaine with Afro-American guys from Boston. A student from Zambia knew the African dance, the 'Quela', which I'd learned in South Africa and he'd learned in Lusaka. Today, thank God, we could dance it together in Cape Town.

Paris opened my eyes to more than Edith Piaf, the Impressionists and snails in garlic butter. I loved it. I still do.

SAME-SAME BUT DIFFERENT

Okechukwu Nzelu

I first went to Rome in the summer of 2018. I was turning thirty a few months later and I was keen to eke out as much joy as possible from my rapidly dwindling twenties. (Other experiences in this vein included living by myself and deciding that I am, indeed, ready for hats.)

I wasn't entirely new to Italy: the previous year, I'd been to Lake Como and spent a day in Milan afterwards where I ate risotto, walked around town and pretended I could afford things. But Rome is different; special. It's famous for so many reasons, and in the weeks leading up to my short holiday I found myself fantasising about all its various attractions: picturesque little streets in picturesque little parts of town, gelato, sunny weather that lasts for more than ninety minutes at a time, gelato, beautiful historic churches, gelato, Caravaggio, gelato . . .

Determined to exercise my independence, I'd spent months doing extra work to pay for the solo holiday – and within days I had spent almost everything I'd saved, and happily so. What I love most about Italy is that there are beautiful things everywhere you turn: the food, the art, the architecture. It's almost overwhelming.

It was my first solo trip, a milestone for me. As excited as I was to follow my own lights, I was also a little anxious – not only about being on my own in a country whose language I could barely understand, but also because I'd read some worrying accounts of overt racism in Italy. Truth be told, when I arrived I was quite taken aback by the starkness of the racial divides in industry: black people could be seen in low-ranking service roles (cleaners, security guards, hawkers) and practically nowhere else. Not in galleries, nor restaurant kitchens, nor bookshops. Italy is not an egalitarian paradise, or a playground where one can escape all of England's problems. But though I felt overlooked or slighted at times, I always felt safe. I could be my twenty-nine-year-old, hat-loving self.

I will always be grateful that Italy offered me a chance to be on my own in a new and exciting place that was also easily navigable; foreign, but still familiar; strange, but safe. One of the best things about Italy – and about most of Europe, by extension – is that it is relatively nearby, culturally not dramatically dissimilar, and yet very much *different*. The food is different; their relationship to food is different. Their artistic history is different; their musical history is different.

Yet it's so close. If I had come from further afield, perhaps, I might have had a different experience. But as someone from Manchester who hadn't travelled extensively, and who was a little nervous about travelling alone, I could encounter some of the most exciting and captivating elements of any city while spending relatively little time and money on flights, swerving jetlag and avoiding a big culture shock. It truly was a kind of freedom.

As a young man on the verge of my thirties (which are pretty great, by the way), I could enjoy my growing self-confidence in a safe environment, not too far from home. For just a few days, I did exactly what I wanted, for as long as I wanted to. It was a deeply special experience for me, and one that I think every young person should be able to have.

And honestly, the gelato really was very good.

'MONSIEUR, NOUS CHERCHONS LA ROUTE . . .'

Ruth Jones

My father Richard *loved* France. In 1946 at the age of eighteen, he travelled on the Golden Arrow train (*La Flèche d'Or*) from Wales to France to stay with Pierre Goujou, his pen-pal, with whom he remained friends well into his eighties. Today we take travel for granted, don't we, audaciously expecting English to be spoken everywhere we go. But imagine travelling to rural France a year after the war, not an easy trip for an eighteen-year-old lad from Neath, with only his schoolboy French for company. I'm so proud of his sense of adventure back then and his keenness to journey beyond the British Isles. Because Dad's love for all things French went on to become infectious – all four of us kids inherited that love. Even today I cannot tell you how excited I get at the prospect of a trip to France. The ferry alone fills me with joy – I LOVE FERRIES. Have done ever since 1971 when we took our first family trip across the English Channel.

Every summer we all squeezed into Dad's Wolsey or Maxi or Princess car and went camping – most years it was France, sometimes Spain or Germany. These holidays engendered in me a love for the exoticism and excitement of *going abroad*, of hearing different languages being spoken, of embracing different cultures, eating different food as well as gifting me the most cherished of family memories, like when my baby sister Maria developed the habit of eating the inside of a baguette when no one was looking, making a bespoke 'bread sock', or putting up the tent in a spectacular thunderstorm or swimming in the glorious Mediterranean – a vibrant sapphire blue that shamed our own dull sea; drinking Orangina with ice and eating fresh crêpes with Nutella – products that weren't on our supermarket shelves back then; attempting to communicate in charade-like mime with kids on the beach who spoke a different language and the delight we felt when we understood each other; visiting sleepy siesta-blessed town squares or the giant Carrefour hypermarkets which sold *everything,* learning how to buy six croissants and a litre of milk *en Français* and generally just being awestruck by the chicness of French life. And when we got lost in France, as we frequently seemed to do, my father – who always welcomed any opportunity to speak French, would stop a passer-by and say '*Monsieur/Madame nous cherchons la route pour . . .*' – it became Dad's holiday catchphrase. And I've never forgotten it – using it on my grown-up trips to France, like a girls weekend in Paris where we got drunk in a tiny French bistro and sung Welsh hymns to a group of Germans, whilst apologising profusely for Brexit; or driving through the sunflower-filled fields near Bordeaux last year en route to a family wedding.

I know we're going to always be European: that we're leaving the European Union, not Europe itself. That I can still catch the ferry to Brittany or sit in the Riviera sun reading novels; visit the vineyards of the Loire or enjoy a bowl of *moules* with a cold French beer, or watch a group of old boys play boules on a Sunday. I know I can still do all those things . . . but it won't be the same, let's face it. It's like being on very good terms with an ex: we may be polite and respectful, even share the odd joke or two. But there will always be that elephant in the room, the fact that we were once together and then we broke up, that the relationship we had broke down. Just so you know, I didn't want us to break up, I wanted to go to Relate; I wanted us to sit down and work out our differences so we could try again. I wanted my dad to ask someone the way, '*Monsieur, nous cherchons la route . . .*'

LUBRIANO

Anna Whitelock

It is precisely because it is unremarkable that Lubriano on the border of Southern Umbria, halfway between Rome and Florence, and with a population of just 900, captures the very essence of the Europe I love. It is here in this tiny medieval village which looks out to the famous hill-top town of Civita di Bagnoregio (called the 'Dying Town' as it is collapsing into the Calanchi Valley below) that I learnt to be a European: to rise early before the sun was hot, to sleep in the afternoon and to eat late in the night, to buy bread twice daily and to look forward to the bitter shot of a morning espresso. It was in Lubriano that I first smelled huge waxy lemons, tasted sun-ripened tomatoes and warm fresh bread made as it has been for years. No labels of 'heritage' or 'authentic' necessary, merely made the way it always had been, always would be. Here in this very ordinary Italian village, I first basked in the warmth of long summer days, sought sanctuary in the cobbled streets and felt the watchful eyes of village elders as they sat on benches and chairs looking on. In Lubriano I grew to love the regular toll of the church bell, the soothing rhythm of the days, the women sweeping their steps and shaking their mats in the cool morning air, the men with scythes on their shoulders heading early to the fields. In Lubriano shops bear no signs, they simply are what they do or what they sell: a hairdresser, the fruit and vegetable shop, a butcher, the baker, the *tabacchi*, a shoemaker and a bar open from dawn to dusk, the beating heart of the village where locals stand to take their morning coffee, or sit in groups sipping tall glasses of beer no matter the time of day. Days stretch long and unhurried, people move slowly, talk for hours, sit and simply watch or wait for nothing in particular. It was ever thus, and will, I'm sure, I hope, always be. A place that time, that politics, hasn't touched, shouldn't touch.

IN PRAISE OF EUROPE'S ZS

Adam Roberts

Z is a wonderful letter: the soothing burr of its sound, the swishy zigzag of its shape, its exotic suggestion of energy ready to uncoil. In English we came to it late, and did not warm to it: 'thou whoreson zed,' snarked Shakespeare in 1600, 'thou unnecessary letter'. In our small-c conservative shore-hugging way, we fight shy of it still, preferring, as it might be, 'customise' to the American-spelling 'customize', and rationing its use in our English words. Its high score in Scrabble – itself indicative of the letter's rare glamour – reflects how rarely appears in English, and when it does crop up it's mostly through loan words from overseas.

But what loan-words! Exciting zoos, thrilling zombies, zealousness and pzazz. That Europe has embraced z in a way Britain hasn't is, I would argue, one more reason to love the continent. Everywhere you look in Europe you find Zs: from Zagreb to Zaragoza; from Zlatan Ibrahimović expertly dribbling his football in Sweden to Slovenian intellectual Slavoj Žižek, whose zs have little hats on them, perhaps to guard them from sunstroke; from Italian piazzas to Circuit Zandvoort in the Netherlands, around which you can zoom-zoom in racing cars. Z is great.

I have a more personal reason for my affection for continental Zs, and that is the French *ville* of Uzès in the department of Gard and the region of Occitanie. This town, with its lovely buzzing name, lies about 25 km north-east of Nîmes, from where the cloth 'denim' originates. I'm wearing denim trousers as I type this, in fact; but Gard as a whole is famous for its cloth production, from durable denims to the fine silks of the Cévennes. Gauze – another beautiful Z-containing word – is part of this French fabricverse: the word is a variant of the Palestinian seaport Gaza, which was famous in the ancient world for its silk production.

My British parents, Francophiles both, bought themselves a small house on the outskirts of Uzès and, upon their retirement, moved there. Age has caused them to sell it now, alas, and to return to this country; but for many years my own family, and the families of my two sisters, would travel down to the south of France every summer. Uzès itself is a wonder: a walled medieval town very largely unspoiled, containing a superb *château du Duché* and central square. In addition to all the obvious reasons to fall in love with the place – the climate, the landscape, the cuisine, the archaeological splendours and cultural richness – is the fact that it manifests a resuscitating logic of *admixture*: as much Spanish or Italian as French, a weaving together of influences that allows the more rebarbative rationalism of the Official French mode to relax a little and breathe. The mistral blows fresh through what might otherwise be oppressive heat. Every now and then a spectacular thunderstorm refreshes the water-table; and then the sun comes out again, bright and strong.

Brexit (that horrid crashing central 'x' like gears grinding) will shuffle us along to the end of the line, turn us into the 'z' with which, by convention, the alphabet ends. It threatens us with that terminal-ness. But alphabets exist in two forms: as a line – like a queue at customs – or in the form it is being deployed here, in this book, as a resource from which all the great literature of the world, Dante and Goethe and Proust and Cervantes as well as Shakespeare and Dickens, is assembled. I hope we can re-centre our whoreson Z, put it back in the middle, where it belongs, where it can flash its sharp adze-blade at dead wood, or buzz pleasantly like a bumble-bee among the flowerbeds. You never know.

Uzès I: Gauze

Mistral in the big tree
blows like rushing water.
Sunlight serves both sky and clouds.

Water can be found in the sky;
and air underground. All
things blended. So: gauze

is half cloth and half atmosphere
each woven in the other; like
lungs stitching air into blood.

Uzès II: Zest

Sunwebs on the pool floor
shudder as if blown by
underwater breezes. Dive into

the shimmer net; its mesh
won't snag your flesh
because light is atoms,

as water is, as stone.
White atoms. One cleanness
washed doubly clean.

Climb from the pool,
dripping on hot stone flags:
the sound of fat frying.

Zest. The sun's wry
glare. Chlorine in my eyes,
the white rush of the wind

rummaging in the leaves of the
fat-headed sycamores, making a noise
exactly like a shower of rain.

ON BREXISTENTIALISM

Ian Martin

Like everyone else I can remember moments of exhilaration in Europe. The personal – a slightly drunken journey down the fire escape of the Pompidou Centre, say. Or the universal – that giddy joy when you're in Rome for the first time and realise it's only the size of Chester Zoo.

But it was Literary Europe that really opened my mind as a teenager. Specifically, Jean-Paul Sartre. Particularly, the *Roads to Freedom* trilogy. I think it was the first time I felt properly European. Something about seeing the exploration of ideas about what it is to be human, to have free will and agency. Existentialism was a great fit for a teenage drop-out, and living in your head is much more interesting if you're swanning around chic Paris cafés with the heavy thinkers and the weighty drinkers.

How different from my boyhood understanding of 'Europe', which had been shaped by the lurid post-war propaganda of action comics, thrilling adventures of uncomplicated selfless British heroes winning the Second World War for a begrudging and frankly undeserving continent. The valiant Brits had character and moral purpose. Europeans were clumped stereotypes. Germans: bullet-headed automatons. Italians: chaotic and comical. French: feckless but romantic allies at the start of war, Vichy quislings when the Nazi occupation took hold.

And it's this period – late-thirties Paris before and after the occupation – that Sartre inhabits in the first book of the trilogy, *The Age of Reason*, through the lives of a group of clever, repellent people. We watch their lives unravel as the promise of personal freedom first collides with the real world and is then obliterated by a new, much worse one. Our anti-hero Mathieu is a philosophy professor who can dazzle sexually available students with his progressive, disruptive views and who is, let's face, it a much better-looking version of Jean-Paul Sartre.

My way in to the novel was via TV. In 1970, when we had just three terrestrial channels in the UK, BBC2 aired David Turner's brilliant and controversial adaptation of the first novel. It was sexually frank, morally confrontational. We heard the characters' private, sordid thoughts. Including those of a terrifying sadomasochist, the flâneur Daniel. More daring still, he was gay.

It caught the zeitgeist. That sense that the old world with its dusty moral certainties and silly national boundaries was about to be overthrown. Young people were thinking the same thing in France as in England, in Spain as in Ireland. We young, adorable, free-loving, forward-looking, *Gitanes*-smoking, novel-reading pioneers – we weren't 'British' any more. The older generation we were pushing against, that sense of entitlement and privilege that claimed an empire, THAT was British. The world WE were about to create would be free, egalitarian, comradely.

From that screening of the *Roads to Freedom* to the 1975 referendum that sent Britain surging into its optimistic European future, I devoured practically everything Sartre had written. I read more European literature. Felt the connectivity of a world about to throw off its shackles. Goodbye and good riddance to my parents' world . . .

And welcome back to my grandparents' world today, apparently. The language of the Brexitistas recalls the propaganda of those boys' comics I read in the fifties. We are encouraged to brace for wartime rationing of resources, to confect a 'Blitz Spirit', to feel a resonance between our exit from Europe and the defeat of Nazism. Even when the tone of anti-Europeanism itself has become strident, nativist, fascistic. Welcome to a weird, inverted Brexistentialist reality where the Nazis hate the Germans.

It will pass, this shuttered xenophobia, as it did before. The deluded war fetishists leading us into a fictionalised past will have to accept that notions of liberty, egality and fraternity can't be contained behind hard borders. That in the end, people will always find new roads to freedom.

ALSO SPRACH SAMADDER

Rhik Samadder

At eighteen I applied to a philosophy course at a prestigious university. I did this partly because 'student of philosophy' sounded like a cool thing to be. (Noun, 1. *Someone who likes to lie in.*) But mostly it was because I had Big Questions. What was I made of? How should we live? Was God really dead, or just having a nap? The place sounded like it might have answers.

When I started the course, however, the British tradition left me cold. It seemed so staid. Peopled with the kind of men you wouldn't want to be stuck with at a wine and cheese. John Locke, father of Liberalism, so sober and methodical. Right about everything, and so boring. David Hume, with his lumpen talk of contiguous causation and inductive scepticism. George Berkeley, who thought nothing existed outside of our perceptions, that it was all just colours and noise. Imagine being sat next to him on the sofa at a party. Although now I think about it, my first year was largely spent in the company of stoners arriving at similar notions.

Thank God – if he was listening – that I also discovered the continental philosophers and assorted weirdos like them. Thinkers from across the Channel whose words made direct sense of my internal world, or else turned it upside down. My favourite was Leibniz. His big, mad idea was that everything was made of monads: jelly-like atoms that reflected the whole universe. He had to redefine the word 'contingent' just to make the theory consistent, which is the kind of balls-out chutzpah I admire. 'Hume is potato,' I remember thinking of one of history's greatest geniuses, 'but Leibniz is a pomegranate.' (In fact, he is a chocolate biscuit.) Heavy metal-moustached Nietzsche was a revelation too. His work contained incredible, *incredible* chapter titles such as 'Why I am So Wise' and 'Why I Write Such Good Books.' It was funnier for being true – they *were* good books, written with epigrammatic brilliance and thundering bombast. Kierkegaard, a pasty Dane swirled with cinnamon and existentialism, wrote about commitment and faith with the intensity they warranted. Heidegger, heavy on the hyphens with his being-in-the-world and being-toward-death, was the Emily Dickinson of the philosophy set (though strangely also a Nazi). Schopenhauer was a poetic miserabilist who made me feel totally isolated in the universe, yet less alone in my head. The freedoms and feminisms of Sartre and de Beauvoir were both frigid and sexy. But no one was as cool as Camus and his popped collar, embracing the absurd. He wasn't so much a man as a thin cigarette, raised like a middle finger.

I'm glad I met that bunch, and we stay in touch. Before them, I didn't think writers could be exciting. I didn't grasp souls had gone before me who were equally disturbed and awestruck at being alive. I didn't know philosophy wasn't just chilly abstraction, that it could be lived and felt and urgent. That the dead could speak to me, and be speaking still. I'm glad they made space on the sofa. Let's not talk politics. Just pass the pomegranate, my friends.

YOU'LL NEVER WALK ALONE

Frank Cottrell Boyce

Dear Europe,

Remember that time in 1973 when Uncle Billy went to watch the Reds beat Borussia Moenchengladbach 3–2 (on aggregate) in the final of the UEFA cup? After the match, the Prussian police herded thousands of ecstatic Scousers onto the waiting charter planes. It was only when he came down to earth with a bump at Liverpool airport that Billy remembered he'd gone to the match in his van. The van that was – he hoped – still neatly parked in the shade of the maples in the Bunter Garten a thousand miles away.

That night was the start of our love affair with Europe. Until then, Liverpool's gaze was fixed the other way – over the sea to Ireland, New York, Valpariso – the old sea routes our fathers had travelled, returning with the monkeys and parrots that played around our tenement balconies long after those trades had stopped.

It was football that bounced Europe into our lives. Liverpool often felt disconnected from the rest of England, but football connected us to Europe like a perfectly weighted pass. Young men who might barely have travelled beyond their own neighbourhoods became familiar with the bus and metro routes of Paris, Rome, Amsterdam and of course Moenchengladbach. I remember sitting in the Liverpool Irish Centre one evening when a whole crowd of slightly merry Dutch fans in orange burst in, saying, 'Irish!? We're with you. Orange and Green, yes?' As though in Ireland the orange and green were just two colours that went together well, rather than the blazons of an ancient blood feud. Everyone cheered them and bought them pints. I ended up driving four of them to Anfield.

That's not to say our story was without pain. I still can't think about Heysel without a spasm of shame and fury. But year after year, young fans came back with new ideas about how to dress – Transalpino was everywhere; how to play football – being thumped by Cruyff's Ajax in Amsterdam in 1966 was the epiphany that illuminated a different kind of football for Shankly – the patient, passing game that carried a whole ideology of teamwork and mutual respect out of the stadium and into the bones of the city. New ideas, too, about what football could mean – seeing how differently the Bundesliga worked with fans and communities illuminated the abusive relationship between Premiership clubs and their 'customers'. The bodies that run the game – UEFA, FIFA, the FA – are bloated bureaucracies vulnerable to corruption and averse to innovation.

Yet the game still delivers moments of sublime beauty and a profound sense of connection. Maybe that's one of the most valuable lessons you taught us – that in a fallen world, there is a price to be paid for the sublime. As Dolly Parton said, if you don't have rain, you don't get rainbows. You don't let that stop you. Utopia is a destination and disillusion is not a reason to cease travelling.

I have lived in France and Spain. I've worked in Italy. But I always end up back here in my hometown. I'm rooted, as Yeats said, in 'one dear perpetual place'. But I hold in my heart a truth that our current leaders are constantly trying to erase – the truth that you can dedicate yourself to one place while revelling in the fact that it is part of something greater, that we never walk alone.

Love and kisses from Liverpool.

SHAKE HELLO, SHAKE GOODBYE

Richard Beard

Before Paris in 1991, the handshake was a source of uncertainty and fear, best avoided. It existed to seal boyish wagers which turned out badly, the handshake a gleeful seal to some deeply unwise agreement. The Anglo-Saxon handshake was essentially insincere, an accepted sign of ownership between football manager and his nervous new signing, or the obligatory photo-opp grab-and-grimace of politicians divided by language and ideology. It permeated business but was tainted by small-man anxieties about the 'strong grip', so much so that insecure management consultants could believe that when two people shake hands, one of them loses.

In the English-speaking world, maybe so. Even the simple handshake could become a cause for despair, like the son and his dad shaking hands as the closest they'd ever get to a hug.

Europe offers a handshake that is both less and more than this. The handshake is ubiquitous and universal, across ages and classes and gender. The first time I went to rugby training in Paris, I shook hands with over thirty different strangers, men and women, players and staff. No one went into the changing rooms until all hands had been shaken. And no one left at the end of the session until the process had been repeated in reverse.

In France, back in the good old days, I shook hundreds of hands every week at work and social events. No arrival or departure, and no other person, was too big or small not to be acknowledged by the courtesy of a handshake; hello handshake, goodbye handshake. All is right with the world.

The Parisian handshake is light (it has to be, it happens so often) and free of the weight of hierarchy. This regular contact is a daily making of the sign of peace, and humbly accepts the tangible physical existence of another human being; present physically, present emotionally. The handshake forms an instant bond, a gender-neutral moment of trust that demonstrates the possibility of touching someone else and coming to no harm.

This is an admirable human achievement, complicated in our cold Northern lives by distance and fear. We must be very frightened. We should shake hands more. The cheek-kiss, for both women and men, can come later. Start with the handshake, graduate to the higher realm of kissing. In the meantime, shake hands with everyone, whoever they are; shake for hello and shake for goodbye, replace the awkwardness of our frozen English farewells with a clear symbol that no grudges will be held and human connection is always possible – after any meeting just as before.

Honestly, I think the universal handshake was catching on. We were learning to reach out, and then the fear came back.

LIVED EXPERIENCE

Tom Chatfield

My mother's partner was born in 1919 and died in 2006. As I get older, I find the life he lived more and more remarkable – in part because so much of it was ordinary for men of his generation. From a provincial background he was plucked into conflict, travelled across half the globe, then made a life in England. And that life helped me to see the world as it was to him: its peace bloodily won, its decency fragile.

He was a psychiatrist, but long before he pursued this specialism he saw service as a medical officer in a tank regiment in the Second World War, landing on D-Day fairly fresh from medical school. He had done a shortened undergraduate course and then his clinical studies in the East End during the Blitz, learning surgical techniques from veterans of the Great War and the Boer War: all the younger men had been called up.

The three of us visited France often when I was young. Once, we went back to Normandy and traced something of the route his regiment had followed as it advanced through towns reduced to rubble. He remembered above all the boredom, the fear and the sheer exhaustion of battle: the night he spent without sleep on a landing craft, offshore, waiting for his turn, the man next to him bleeding to death from a shrapnel wound. After the landing, when they had finally secured the beach, he fell asleep under an armoured vehicle and only awoke when it drove off.

My education in the 1980s and 1990s, in a typically English way, involved few encounters with living cultures other than my own. It was hard to connect the few sentences of French I learned to write at school with the foreign country we drove through, stopping for crêpes and mini-golf. And it was impossible to connect my first few trips to Spain with anything I'd learned at school, where history started with Roman villas, ended in a blur of trenches and Wilfred Owen, and barely touched the Iberian peninsula. The idea that history was also lived experience came slowly, creeping up on me as we travelled, returned, talked.

A few months before he died, I typed up as many of his memories as he could manage to dictate. He talked about the combat he'd seen as they advanced east from Normandy and he tried to patch up men thrown around inside their tanks by shell blasts. There was little he could do, barely any way even to ease their pain, and that haunted him.

As the war in Europe ended, he was posted to Burma – but he never made it. In Poona, he was intercepted by a Major who wanted to make up two pairs for whist (or so he always said). His regiment then demobbed via West Africa, from where many of the troops were drawn. Eventually, fresh from the army, he found a position as ship's surgeon on the Paraguay Star, which sailed to and from Buenos Aires for the Blue Star Line. It was a wonderful time in his life – a world away from the grey England of rationing and rebuilding. He returned with luggage full of meat and eggs from the galley: he'd performed successful surgery on a steward after an on-board accident and found himself a great favourite among the crew.

It was during these few post-war years that he learned to love the

Spanish language – and that he began to think of himself as cosmopolitan, or at least someone with a deep feeling for places that others called home. He was a shy man, but one of the great virtues of his life (as I now see it) was the degree to which he overcame the crutches of conventional-mindedness when choosing his path. His parents had been ignorant of foreign parts; the little schools he'd attended had taught Empire and glory. He had unlearned, carefully, these old lessons.

As a psychiatrist and a conversationalist, he was above all someone who didn't judge hastily. I loved this about him. He created spaces within which you could explain yourself. When friends came to the house, he asked them how they were and what they were doing – and then he listened to their answers, and asked them to explain things further. He didn't presume or pronounce. He took an interest in both sides of a story. He spoke slow, beautiful Spanish and played Argentine tangos from old LPs.

Eventually, for me, the Europe we visited became the idea that everything I was taught to take for granted could be seen another way: that things near and obvious to me were distant and strange to others. That learning to explain things in different ways, with different words, was the essence of understanding them with any kind of fidelity to lived experience.

He introduced me to Europe, and with it to the idea that what I didn't know was vastly more interesting and important than what I did.

A RAINY MORNING IN MARCH

Liane Jones

A rainy morning in March 1972, and everything felt tall and vertical: the trees along the river bank, the iron gates, the white school building like a faded wedding cake, perched on steps at the top of the drive, the rain blowing in rivulets down the sides of the school buses. The pupils were swarming in through the gates in various stages of hurry and loitering. They all seemed to be dressed differently, in free interpretations of the dress code, and the voices that detached themselves from the babble were in a baffling range of tones and accents. Walking with a thirteen-year-old's self-consciousness in the middle of the surge, I looked at the haphazard crowd around me and felt astonishment. It hadn't occurred to me that moving to France would be like this.

We'd come for two years with my father's job and we'd been in the country a few days, blinking at the many ways in which the small town of Le Vésinet, just outside Paris, was foreign – the low houses with red roofs, the tall ones rearing up like squeezed châteaux, the small lakes that dotted the residential roads, the bing-bing-BING melody played in the local Prisunic, the lemon-flavoured chewing gum, the teenagers who rode to the *lycée* on puttering *mobylettes*. Every vista of the town – the cinema, the rectangular market square, the sky above the railway line – struck with me with peculiar clarity: the smallest things seemed heightened, it was hard not to register detail. I've experienced the same thing since, at other times of dislocation – sometimes when under strain, sometimes when very happy, but I'm not sure if I've ever known it so intensely as during those early days in France.

That morning, as my brother and I set off for our new school, I knew I had a stiff adjustment to make. The school was an English-speaking one with daily compulsory French, and I was braced for a cross between an English grammar, an English boarding school and a French finishing school, a place that would perform a sort of human embroidery, threading English pupils through the eye of French culture. Instead, on that soaking gravel drive, hearing my new classmates swear in numerous languages, my preconceptions dissolved. I didn't know what I was stepping in to but it was obviously something multiparous and untidy.

The 'English School' was a joyous experience for me. Its students came from all over the world: some of us were first-timers at being abroad, others were seasoned at moving on, following their pilot or journalist or military parents from post to post. I learned to love France in their company – Saturday mornings at the local ice rink, trips to each others' homes after school, then, as I got a little older, group get-togethers on a Friday night in Paris, when we'd meet in the fluorescent tunnels of the Étoile metro station and climb together up the steps into the navy blue night with the Arc de Triomphe next to us and the Champs Élysées and other great avenues radiating out. And the school itself is stamped in my memory – I feel as if it's stamped in my flesh: the black-and-white tiles of the hall, pale grey panelling, the hooters sounding from barges going by on the Seine; the glamorous school secretary with heavily mascara-ed lashes, who used to be the head girl; the vat of hot chocolate the cooks made in winter, into which we'd dip our tin mugs; the small classrooms on the top floor with little windows in the mansard roof, where the sun pooled in summer.

It was an experience both insular and open: because we were uprooted, and fairly transient (hardly anyone was in the country for more than three years), we relied on each other for the majority of our friendships and activities; at the same time, these friendships provided continual surprises, because we were from so many different backgrounds. Every day we'd be taken aback – by reactions to small things such as food, clothes, jokes; by deeper matters such as how we talked about parents and families; and then occasionally very stark differences would emerge. For example, some people's families were in France not as working expats but as political exiles or refugees, and there were sensitivities over geopolitics – India and Pakistan, the Maghreb, Israel–Palestine; I remember an angry scuffle between two boys over the last, on the stairs to the basement cloakrooms. I wasn't well informed about such things, and often didn't know what to make of them. The dissonances lodged in my mind, seeding curiosity; later, in adulthood, they would come back to me, and I would be moved to go and find out more. When I look at the things I've chosen to research and write about, I can see most of them foreshadowed here.

One would bring me back to France itself – fourteen years on, I would return to trace the stories of SOE agents, ordinary civilians who had been infiltrated into the country during the Second World War to work with the Resistance. The research took me to different regions of France, often to places I'd visited with my family on our regular let's-explore jaunts. Being introduced into the homes of former *résistants*, by then in their seventies, and trying to find fields where weapons had been parachuted in, and buildings that had hidden radio operators, listening to them talk about the occupation, it felt like time travel, passing underneath my own encapsulated memories to try and lift some of the layers that I had sensed existing around me, but been too young to understand.

Did I know the 'real' France at all in those teen years? Probably not. Most of us in that rootless (and regularly changing) bunch knew that we could only claim a passing-through existence. At the end of two and a half years, I couldn't even speak fluent French – it would take various trips and concerted efforts in my twenties before I became at all conversational. Would it be exaggerating to say that my time there taught me how interconnected the world is? After all, it was currents of history, trade, war, diplomacy and politics that brought us from so many different places to study the English curriculum on the banks of the Seine and play pinball in *café-tabacs* . . . Although it's only with hindsight that it becomes clear, I think I did get my first sense of it there. It was, if not a French education, perhaps a European one, and I will always be grateful for it.

THE WIDENING OF MY WORLD

Onjali Q. Raúf

On my tenth birthday, I was given a gift that changed my world: my very own atlas to do with as I wanted. It wasn't as fancy as the huge coffee-table-sized one my mum had which I was never allowed to touch, but it was all mine. Mine to make plans with just as I wished!

And boy did I!

That atlas replaced my toys and all my reading books in one fell swoop. I carried it with me wherever I went. I fell asleep with it in bed. I took it into school every day for at least half a year, and bored my poor friends with stories of all the journeys I was going to make.

Journeys that always, at every moment of imagining, began with Europe.

I have no idea how or who planted the seed in my mind, but imaginings of travelling to France, Italy, Greece and Spain with nothing but a backpack and a friend have been with me ever since I can remember. Perhaps it was seeded by my mum, who always dreamed of going to Paris one day and standing atop the Eiffel Tower. Or it might have been the friends I had at primary school – one of whom had lived in Rome for a year and who I desperately wished I could be. Or maybe the tanned neighbours who would occasionally drop by with a box of French *macarons* or sundried olives. How it got there I suppose doesn't really matter: the fact is the seed was planted and was growing strong, and has never left me.

Will never leave me.

The Berlin Wall fell when I was eleven; I remember my mum screaming at the telly with tears in her eyes. At thirteen I told my form teacher that I wanted to work for the United Nations – if for no other reason than it would mean lots of travelling! At fifteen, I was devastated at not being allowed to go on a French exchange trip to visit my pen-pal. (For some reason, my family thought a short, chubby, East London teen was at risk of being kidnapped anywhere outside Britain!)

But at age seventeen, I was allowed to head to Germany as part of a college history trip. It was my first ever venture to Europe, and I know I didn't sleep the night before. I can remember the thrill of pulling out my passport to be checked by a border officer, and it coming back with a special sticker proving I had entered Germany and showing the date by which I had to leave. I remember marvelling at the beauty of the buildings and palaces that our coach rushed past, at the fact that people were driving on the 'wrong side' of the road, and the feel of the different money that was so exotic to the touch.

Growing up and heading to universities in Wales and, then, Oxford, I boarded with students from every corner of Europe. Students who started off as strangers, then became dear friends. Friends who stayed up talking politics, feminism and movies with me deep into our pre-examination and dissertation nights. Friends who welcomed me into their homes and families, and still continue to do so two decades later. Friends who I now work with in the refugee camps of Calais and Dunkirk. In short, friends I cannot imagine my life without, and who have opened up my world, my taste buds, my eyes to sights, viewpoints, and understandings I would otherwise never have had.

My childhood atlas has long since disappeared, but the adventures I planned on having in the wider world, which always began with Europe, go on. Because Europe is a part of me. Always has been. Forever will be.

GORBACHEV ON THE A299

Gabby Hutchinson Crouch

I'm driving my son and his three best friends to a climbing centre for his birthday and chatting with a ten-year-old about Chernobyl. He's happy to sit in the front and avoid the Fortnite talk going on in the back, opting instead to talk to me about his interests in geopolitics and cars. He is Polish, and his dad has told him all about growing up a few hundred miles from the site of the nuclear disaster.

He blithely chats to me about his parents' childhoods in the Soviet Union. It isn't the first time it's hit home to me how people who are now friends and peers via my children grew up in a world that was, at the time, utterly alien to me. When I was a kid, people from the other side of the Iron Curtain were presented as either fearsome or pitiable, as in those well-intentioned but patronising *Blue Peter* campaigns featuring gaunt Chernobyl children (the mysterious and unfortunate Them) and Bring & Buy sales run by pudgy-kneed schoolchildren (the normal and benevolent Us).

I think about how much has changed since then – not simply for this kid in the front seat, his attention whizzing between decrying Trump and pointing out a Mazda that's impressed him – but for my own family. When I was at school in Derbyshire in the eighties, I considered myself fairly exotic on the grounds that I was Welsh. One time we had a Q&A with a teacher about what it was like to live in a strange and foreign land, because we'd heard that she'd been in France for a bit. So my childhood was not one rich with variation of cultural background or perspective. I had to wait until I went to university in the late nineties to befriend peers who had come from different countries, and immediately asked them to teach me some swear-words in their mother tongue, as is tradition.

Thirty years on, even growing up in a distinctly suburban corner of East Kent, my children's friendships have been very different. They've been surrounded with friends from all over the globe at school and have, I'm sure, picked up some brilliant swear-words as a result, as well as different perspectives – a more globalised worldview than the one I grew up with. I want my children to have it better than I did, and in this regard, I believe that they've been gifted a far richer pool of experience, through absolutely no extra effort on my part, which is nice.

I consider telling my son's friends that our carpool is remarkably multinational, then realise that for these four guileless Gen Zers it's not remarkable at all. Nor should it be. Instead, I start talking about my memories of the Berlin Wall coming down, but by this point my friend in the front has seen a Jaguar, and so the topic of conversation has moved on.

Oh well.

AN ARTISTIC EDUCATION

Janet Gleeson

In 1973, keen to put school behind me and experience something beyond the Home Counties, I found a job as an au pair in Paris. The family turned out to be friendly, work wasn't demanding and the children were naughtily enjoyable. Sundays were free and, at first, with little money and no friends, there was time to be filled. One day my employer Philippe, an architect, told me that the Louvre was free on Sundays. From the first time I walked through those great doors, my life changed, and I got into a habit that didn't alter much over the next nine months. Breakfast, a short metro ride, at the gallery for opening time.

The Louvre was quite different from anything I had seen before – each visit was a new adventure. First, I encountered works of art that were familiar from books I'd read: the *Venus de Milo* within touching distance; the *Mona Lisa* seen up close before the crowds arrived. More exciting were the unfamiliar things: the bizarre eroticism of *Gabrielle d'Estrees* and her nipple-pinching sister; the tranquillity of Chardin's still lives; the disconcerting acres of colourful dimpled flesh in the Rubens gallery; the desperate drama of Gericault's *Raft of the Medusa* and Ingres' sensually exotic scene in *The Turkish Bath*. When I look back, there was a lot of painterly flesh on show, something novel and exciting to my teenage eyes, but

179

even now, four decades on, I still feel the impact of these experiences.

Over those nine months of Sundays I explored in my own time a wealth of European art from the Middle Ages onwards and in the process prepared myself for university. Although I did not know it at the time, those visits also laid the foundations for my future life and career. I became an art historian, a paintings expert at an auction house, a writer and, above all else, a European.

THE BORGHESE GALLERY

Abi Curtis

There's a gallery that lies among formal gardens on the outskirts of Rome that houses some of the most amazing sculptures in the world. I first went there while backpacking around Italy with my student friend Kate from Chicago. Grubby, tired but enchanted by all of Italy, I found myself captivated by a Gian Lorenzo Bernini sculpture created in the 1620s. It is inspired by Ovid's *Metamorphoses* from AD 8, that text of human-natural transformations, by turns horrifying and beautiful, that has inspired centuries of art and literature.

As a writer, I have realised that what interests me the most about narrative is the possibility of transformation: the pain of loss coupled with its power to move life on. This sculpture captures that. Daphne is pursued by Apollo, who wants her despite her desperate resistance. She is saved, after a fashion, by the pity of the gods, and is turned into a laurel tree just as Apollo lays his hands on her. Bernini has captured her in mid-transformation, delicate leaves sprouting from her fingertips, her look of surprise and anguish, the dynamic, baroque twisting of her supple body soon to be sealed in bark. Apollo looks tender and defeated, so close to grasping the object of his desire. Nobody really wins, but nature comes to claim Daphne as its own. When the sculpture was restored, they found the marble leaves so delicately carved that when they struck them with a tuning-fork they made a sound like crystal. I wondered how anyone could work such an unrelenting material into such fluidity, dynamism and fleshy reality.

On the train to Assisi, my friend and I had seen the Altissimo mountain where Michelangelo got his marble for *David* and the *Pietà*. In the distance, as the train clattered by, we had thought it tipped with snow, but that was the white marble, veining down into dark grey. We didn't feel the minor tremor of the earth because of our rickety train. Just a year before, Assisi had suffered an earthquake that had cracked the walls of its Basilica, destroying its Giotto frescoes from the late thirteen-century and terrifying its inhabitants and visitors. By the time we reached Assisi, the tourists had left, fearing it may happen again. We didn't figure it out for a couple of days, enjoying the place almost to ourselves and the lavish hospitality of our host family, who were so grateful we had not fled.

I look back and think about the hard delicacy of the marble, the fragility of the earth. I think of Venice, threatened regularly by submersion, or Pompeii with its ashy outlines of loved ones clinging to one another as they burned. Pisa's charmingly leaning tower built on unstable ground, or the Cinque Terre's crumbling cliffs with its pastel houses clinging to the edges. I remember a visit to Leonardo da Vinci's *Last Supper*, whose painted plaster is so delicate the very breaths of its awed viewers are degrading it. I find such beauty in that fragility, as did Bernini – catching people between desire and loss and celebrating the transformation that results.

MY NORTH, MY SOUTH, MY EAST AND WEST

DEVOTIONS UPON EMERGENT OCCASIONS

Shami Chakrabarti

No man is an island,
Entire of itself,
Every man is a piece of the continent,
A part of the main . . .*

It was the late eighties and my long vacation from law studies at the LSE. I worked as a short order cook in the newly opened coffee shop 'Importers' in Golders Green. 'Short order' is a conveniently polite definition of the limit of my culinary skills – then as now, thirty years on. Colette was our manager and she hailed from Ireland. French Sarah and Marie waited tables and there were many others whose names have sadly faded. I was born in London of Indian parents, but we were all young Londoners full of curiosity for our city and the wide world beyond. We spent much of our spare time together, in bedsits and shared houses. Marie, a Goth, would play Nick Cave and bring slightly better wine than I would have known to choose *pour le fromage.*

Then one day, Sarah became bored or homesick or both. She was taking off for her mother's house in the South of France and I was invited. I had already been to Paris several times, had a French A-Level and a little reading of Camus, Sartre and de Beauvoir. Yet there is nothing quite like the opportunity to stay with a family, sharing their food, shelter and stories. That kindness – repeated many times in the years that followed – helped shape me. I'll never forget arriving in the beautiful medieval village-centre late at night with my friend. The sound of the summer crickets was rudely interrupted by Johnny Marr's jangly guitar (Sarah's little sister was desperate to go to Manchester). Wanderlust was clearly in the family DNA, with grandparents originally from Russia and Italy. As the artist-mother of these young women conjured supper, I remarked (in my best school French) that I had never seen tomatoes so red. She replied that it was a small miracle that there were any tomatoes in England. She winked and we laughed together.

Some months later Anya, a German friend and fellow law student, invited a few of us, first to her home in Frankfurt and then to Berlin to celebrate New Year's Eve. What a night. During the day there were all sorts of restrictions on how to cross the divide via the Brandenburg Gate or Checkpoint Charlie, depending on your nationality. As midnight approached, the sheer numbers of revellers made petty policing redundant. I found myself hauled up by human hydraulics and then, moments later, I was in the East. I went home to London with beautiful graffitied chips from the once so brutally permanent wall that was not to last the year.

Now I am fifty. I love the United Kingdom as much as anyone, not least for being the home that my adventurous, departed parents chose. But even our most patriotic and celebrated cultural heritage appears to need Danish Princes as much as Scottish Thanes; to revel in Burgundy and Bach as much as Elgar and Pale Ale.

And there is no adventure or learning without the seas and borders crossed and the meals and stories shared.

If a clod be washed away by the sea,
Europe is the less . . .*

*(From 'No Man is an Island' by John Donne, 1572–1631)

THE WORLD IN A BOOK

Michael Wood

Years ago, as a graduate student, I got the precious green reader's ticket allowing me to enter the students' room of the British Museum and to handle manuscripts, some of our greatest treasures. The first book I ordered was a ninth-century book of psalms. It is tiny, 125x90mm, intended to be portable, for daily use, and it has all the signs of being well used, along with the marks of its later journeys and adventures. It was written in Rheims in Carolingian minuscule, the most beautiful and practical Western hand ever devised; a script developed during Europe's first renaissance under Charlemagne when an English scholar Alcuin headed his think-tank. The book later travelled to Italy with one of Charles's descendants, but by around 900 it was in England, and I have often wondered whether it was perhaps brought there by Alfred the Great, who made two visits to Rome when he was a child. Later it belonged to Alfred's grandson Athelstan, the first king of all the English, a man whose European ties were second to none among English rulers. He made European marriage alliances, fostered European princes, sent a pan-British embassy to Rome to receive the pallium; and despatched a great embassy to visit 'all the churches of Germany' – a very special link as it had been Anglo-Saxon missionaries who had converted the Germans in the eighth century. In his polylingual court were scholars from Ireland, France and Germany. And the little psalter is the fruit of those exchanges. Athelstan had additions made which tell us how he and his court saw the world. There's an Irish calendar listing saints from Britain, Brittany, France and Italy; a gorgeous set of Latin collects written in Rome in the 400s, and prayers in accurate Greek written in Latin letters, including an Antiochene litany of saints which, one assumes, came with Theodore, the Greek-speaking Archbishop of Canterbury who had been educated in Syria, and abbot Hadrian, 'a man of African nation'. Both these former refugees had imbibed Latin culture in Italy in the 600s, and came to England where they became the most influential figures in English educational history.

Out of such diverse European and Mediterranean threads the pattern of our own culture has been woven. After the fall of Rome the peoples of the Barbarian West, Anglo-Saxons, Franks, Goths, Germans, built their new societies with all the optimism of migrants thrown up on strange shores. But they did it with the absolute conviction that they belonged to the cosmopolis of Christian, Latin, Europe. For the English, Gregory the Great, who sent the conversion mission of 597 to Canterbury, was 'our foster father', and they never forgot him.

The English may have been physically divided from Europe by the Channel. Playing with the medieval encyclopaedists' definition of the 'tripartite world', they liked to say they were an *alter orbis,* another world, 'out on the edge'. But in a deep cultural sense they were part of Europe, as Alcuin said, fed by the 'nourishing streams of the Hebrews', the 'light out of Africa' and the wisdom of Latin Christendom; all drawn together by the first renaissance of Charlemagne 'Father of Europe', from which our later renaissances grew. For the historian, we are all children of Charlemagne. My love letter then is to everything this little book stands for – the deep ties of culture, the exchanges of knowledge and learning, the evolution of justice, and even early ideas of human rights through Christian humanism. Without Europe, who are we?

EUROLINGUISTIC UNION

David Crystal

My first visit to the Europe over the seas was when I was an undergraduate, and I spent a summer at a youth camp in the Alps, for an organisation called Concordia. The task was to build a bridge across a river. There were about twenty of us from different countries. It was the moment I realised that not everyone who spoke French spoke it the way I'd learned it in school. A couple of the lads were Algerians, and their usage was fascinatingly different from the Parisian version I'd been told was the correct one.

The experience fuelled my growing love affair with languages. I'd come across dialects and accents before, of course, having grown up in Wales and moving to Liverpool, and then London, so I knew English had a great deal of variation, but nobody had ever told me there were different kinds of French, expressing an intriguing range of identities.

I should have guessed. During my first year reading English at University College London, I had been introduced to the Germanic family of languages to which English belongs, and learned some Gothic, Old Norse, and Frisian. I was also introduced to comparative philology, and the discovery in the eighteenth century that most of the languages of Europe were related in one huge Indo-European family. The metaphor of the 'family' appealed to me, and the associated notions of 'parent', 'mother', and 'daughter' languages. Languages were feminine, evidently, like ships, and (I learned in the Alps) wheelbarrows (*brouettes*). It seemed that I should not just study them. The metaphor suggested I should love them too.

That wasn't difficult. Languages mean peoples and peoples mean cultures and cultures mean differences, and it was always the differences that I fell in love with. And what a fine linguistic playground Europe was – and is. The European bit of Indo-European was the most practicable place to start, and it wasn't long before I found out – discovery within discoveries – that not all the languages of Europe belonged to that family. Basque, for instance; an isolated survivor from an age that pre-dated the arrival of the Indo-Europeans. One of the great mysteries in the history of language. For a while I collected number systems, but counting from one to ten in Basque was nothing like any of the other languages I knew (*bat, bi, hiru, lau* . . .).

Europe is like that. Turn a corner and a new language or accent or dialect greets you – especially these days, with so many world cultures present through immigration. I later became a specialist in English language studies, but Europe was always there. Of the over 600,000 words in the *Oxford English Dictionary*, about eighty per cent of them come from non-Germanic languages, with Latin, Greek, French, Spanish and Italian being leading contributors. There was a linguistic union long before the political one, which will remain, whatever else happens. And whenever I explore a new production on the English language stage, I know the languages and peoples and cultures of Europe are waving to me from the wings.

PIZZA AND THE CHANNEL TUNNEL

Kate Williams

In 1964, Britain and France agreed to build a tunnel under the Channel. In January 1973, with the confirmation of EEC membership, the second stage of *Le Tunnel* planning was complete. But two years later, it was cancelled – then restarted in the 1980s as the 'Mousehole project'.

But there had been talk of a Tunnel long before the 1960s. The first plans in 1802 coincided with the brief peace of Amiens in the Napoleonic Wars between England and France. Albert Mathieu Favier designed a huge tunnel, big enough for horses and carriages, with giant chimneys rising above the sea to bring in air. It would be lit by oil lamps and there would be a mid-tunnel island – above sea level! – for changing horses. Napoleon was most interested in the idea but abandoned it when war broke out once more. In 1881, the plans were revisited and both sides built a pilot tunnel of nearly two thousand metres on each side. But the Channel Tunnel refused to go away. Even Winston Churchill produced a newspaper essay in 1936 titled 'Why Not a Channel Tunnel?' and in 1955, both sides began determinedly exploring the possibility of a tunnel.

On 6 May 1994, the Queen and François Mitterand opened the Tunnel. The Queen whizzed through in her Rolls-Royce Phantom from France to the UK in thirty-two minutes: three minutes faster than had been promised. As the *Guardian* put it, 'with every British journey closer to the heart of Europe, Europe gets closer to the heart of the British: with inexorable and hopeful consequences for us all'.

I remember my first trip on it. 'They don't tell you you're going through the tunnel! It just goes black!' I reported back most excitedly. It seemed absolutely astonishing to me.

The nineties saw Britain and Europe ever closer, in social, political and geographical terms. With the Eurostar, the car trains through the tunnel and the explosion of cheap flights, travel to Europe was easier and cheaper than ever before. Our interest in European culture exploded. And – how can I put it politely? – we Brits began to eat proper European food. As the *Guardian* had pointed out in the same article in 1994, 'Paris for lunch for Londoners also meant London for lunch for Parisians'. But we had a bit of learning to do in terms of food . . .

Growing up in the Midlands, we didn't do too well when it came to European food. There was no French food and the only stab at it we had was Italian – and, well, it wasn't really very Italian. Take pizza. Our mixture of cheese, tomato and dough was special in its own way. For me, either it was a cookery class in school, where we used scone dough with tomato purée and grated cheddar on top, or it was a Findus frozen baguette pizza at a friend's house.

There wasn't much else on offer at that time, in that place. I asked my UK followers on twitter what their first pizza experience was, got nearly eight hundred answers and my conclusion is that there was good pizza in London and some cities with an Italian quarter or good-sized Italian population – such as Isola Bella in Manchester, begun by Evandro Barbieri who came from

Milan as a waiter and later received the equivalent of a knighthood from Italy. As for the rest of us . . . we had frozen pizza, or made our own out of crumpets, baguettes or scone dough – or even what was essentially bread, covered in tomato purée and then cheddar. And frankly, our pasta wasn't much better – with an enthusiasm for pasta bakes that involved cooked pasta mixed with mushroom soup and sweetcorn and cheddar on top.

After all, it wasn't so long before that the TV-watching population been thrilled in 1957 by a BBC *Panorama* film of people in Switzerland harvesting spaghetti from trees – delighted to have such a bumper crop due to the 'virtual disappearance of the spaghetti weevil'. A Dimbleby voiceover made it seem even more authentic, even though it was broadcast on 1 April and hundreds of people rang in with questions about cultivating their own spaghetti. The BBC advice was to 'place a sprig of spaghetti in tomato sauce and hope for the best'.

The first Pizza Hut opened in 1973, providing a very US pizza (as late as the mid-eighties, they were still running television ads making it clear that it was OK for a British clientele to use a knife and fork, rather than eat with their fingers like a decadent American). Many Brits watched a pizza arrive in *ET* in 1982, questioning what it even was.

As a teenager, I went to visit my Italian pen pal, who lived just outside Venice. Her mother made us pizza on my first night. It was a revelation. Light dough, high-quality toppings carefully weighed out. Ever since, it has been the taste of Italy for me. I even bought some pizza-making kits home to share with my family, but they were seized at Birmingham airport, as they apparently looked like drugs.

Of course there was Pizza Express, first opened in 1965 in

London's Soho, but it was out of reach for most people, and it wouldn't be until the nineties that it assumed the high-street dominance we now associate it with. Then there was olive oil replacing sunflower as the staple oil in your average British kitchen. And everyone from Nigella to Jamie Oliver showing us how to cook authentic Italian food – and even Delia Smith in 1993 popularising the recipe for Pasta Puttanesca or 'lady of the night's pasta', with chilli and anchovies, dubbed so she decided because the taste was 'hot, strong and gutsy'.

Italian food has definitely taken over the UK, but it's not just pizza. The cuisine of this country has been deeply affected by the influence of our European cousins, as well as the rest of the world. From paninis to pasta, from baguettes to bratwurst, from chorizo to cheese, we've taken the best of the food of our continent and made it available everywhere, while still celebrating our own home-grown produce. It's indicative of the joy that comes when we collaborate with our neighbours and look outwards.

THROUGH THE ARCHED WINDOW

Philip Ardagh

I never set foot in continental Europe until adulthood. Childhood holidays were always spent in England on beaches and moorland, visiting medieval churches along the way. The 'tock' of the latch lifted on a south door, and the musty odour of ancient wood and stone and damp were, and remain, a familiar constant. I didn't think of Normans as inhabitants of Normandy but as a style of architecture with round arches, later outdated by pointed Gothic. Yes, 1066 and all that turned them into chain-mailed soldiers with flattened nose-guards (and, for a while, I even lived within half a day's march of the site of the Battle of Hastings) but actually visiting Normandy – seeing the castle built on the site of William the Bastard's fort; seeing the Bayeux Tapestry and knowing it was probably embroidered by many an English hand (and is set to return to Britain in 2022) – brought everything into focus. Couple this with my first sighting of the remains of the mulberry harbours just off the Normandy beaches, there since the D-Day landings, and it confirmed our bond through common blood, in our veins and on the battlefield. And it's not just Normandy. It's not just France. At a time of division, I want to embrace the Greece of Perseus and Aphrodite; the Holland of windmills and Rembrandt, the Spain of flamenco and Gaudi; the Italy of Caesar and olive oil; the Germany of Goethe. Their history is our history. This is a true relationship for life. This is love.

OUR SHARED PAST

Nick Barratt

I am a historian of medieval English history. How can I not love Europe?

Durham cathedral provided my first knowing encounter with European culture. There, I was moved and awed by the majesty of the imposing architecture – brought to England by the Normans – which struck me as a physical embodiment of medieval power, providing shelter and protection inside its walls for culture, knowledge and learning.

Fusing Scandinavian genes with Frankish culture, the Normans were a hybrid European people who carved out their place in a landscape still haunted by the remnants of the lost Roman world: politics were still dominated by a Holy Roman Emperor, and it was the Pope, based in Rome, who safeguarded Europe's spiritual needs (hence the term 'Romanesque' to describe Durham cathedral's architecture).

The Norman Conquest is often seen as the suppression of the 'English' by the French. However, the Anglo-Saxons were themselves invaders, their ancestors migrating to our shores as the Roman Empire fell, pushing the native Britons from their homelands. We have always been a home to populations born elsewhere – Jewish financiers who came over with the Normans, Italian bankers who took up the financial reins after Edward I expelled the Jews, Huguenot weavers fleeing religious persecution, German and Polish settlers escaping political turmoil, Eastern European Jews forced to leave their homes during the Russian pograms, Belgians evacuated to our country as the Great War broke out. All of these people have assimilated into British life, reinforcing the fact that we are all unequivocally and inescapably European.

I have a fascination with the Plantagenet kings of England that has no doubt played a part in why Normandy feels like a second home to me. I love to explore the beautiful countryside, rivers and coast with my family, perhaps in part because they are so familiar. A sleepy Norman village has a similar feel to its counterpart in the south of England; it is very easy to recall the fact that we share a common history, often hidden.

Take Tinchbray, in lower Normandy, for example. There is no reason why anyone should have heard of this small town of only a few thousand inhabitants – there are prettier or more famous places to visit. Yet in the nearby fields, two sons of William the Conqueror fought a momentous battle in 1106. The younger son, Henry I of England, defeated his older brother Robert, Duke of Normandy, and united the two realms, with consequences that would play out over the next few centuries.

I felt a growing sense of excitement as we drove closer, at the thought that we were visiting a place that was central to English history. There was no discernible memorial to mark the battlefield; only a medieval historian, perhaps, would recognise its significance. Yet, doubtless, many of the people living there today share common ancestors with large numbers of people across the Channel. We have the same history, bloodlines, culture, traditions.

For the last two years, we have visited Brittany, another region closely connected over many centuries with the British Isles – most notably Cornwall, sharing more than just rugged coasts and small fishing villages. Since Roman times, people have migrated between Cornwall and Brittany, leaving behind many common words and similar place names. Even the untrained eye can spot some of the shared cultural links. While strolling through the marketplace and old streets of Dinan we encountered Alain Salaver playing his hurdy-gurdy and singing old Breton folk songs that had echoes of their English counterparts. Listening to him play was to step back in time, and somehow the difference in language served only to reinforce the similarities. My two-year-old daughter was spellbound.

There are countless other areas that share cultural, social or economic links with Europe. In the sixteenth century, Dutch settlers drained large parts of East Anglia and the Fens to return them to cultivation; today, many of the farms still require large numbers of migrant workers from Eastern Europe to pick the crops. London's position as the financial heart of Europe can be traced back to the Italian banking houses of the Riccardi and Frescobaldi in the thirteenth century, enjoying trading privileges in the City in return for cash that underwrote the military campaigns of Edward I. There are numerous examples of European influence across music and art, particularly as the Renaissance swept across the continent.

The frustrations with the European Union expressed today by large sections of the population are, of course, not the same as a resentment towards Europe as a whole. It's reminiscent of the scene from *Life of Brian* where John Cleese's character asks, 'What have the Romans ever done for us?' to be met by a long list of achievements that embrace the whole spectrum of human endeavour, ending most poignantly with peace. We have had several 'Brexits' since the Romans abandoned their outermost province – the loss of Normandy in 1204, the expulsion of English settlers in France between 1448 and 1453, the break with Rome in 1534 – and each one has been followed by a period of uncertainty and instability. There are worrying similarities with the situation today, insomuch as the last two occasions were met with mass protests against fundamental changes to society – Cade's revolt in 1450 and Robert Aske's 'pilgrimage of grace' in 1536. It feels as though we are living through a similar convulsion to our established way of life. We should try, therefore, to take comfort in the fact that on each occasion we have recalled our essential ties with our friends and neighbours across the Channel and found common cause – usually through the arts, the means by which we express our common humanity.

So let me rephrase my opening lines. I am a historian of medieval European history. How can I not remain optimistic?

MY FAMILY AND OTHER FOREIGNERS

Simon Callow

57 Varieties, my grandmother used to call us, after the famous Heinz slogan. Her grandfather, Henry Otto Fleuss, was from Düsseldorf, her mother Welsh. Her husband, my grandfather, was Danish; his mother French.

When my mother married things got more complicated. My father's mother, Toto, was French, or, more precisely, Franco-Scottish: her father was a Scotsman who had gone to live in Lyon as a teenager, where he met my great-grandmother, Mémé. Mémé was Swiss; she later divorced him, then spent over twenty years in Algeria as a governess, before finally ending up in Britain in her early seventies. After a quarter of a century of living here in St John's Wood, with my great aunt Titi, she spoke no word of English, happily spending the day looking at pictures of Paris on a device called a Stereopticon, which gave her 3D images of a city she barely knew.

My grandmother Toto, Mémé's eldest daughter, arrived in England as a young bride when she was barely twenty, fluent in English, but to the day she died she spoke the language with an accent which made Inspector Clouseau seem like an effortless linguist. Her social circle was largely made up of fellow immigrants – Fifi Brebis, Lily Weiss, Germaine Eustace – who seemed to me to come from the pages of *Clochemerle*. When Toto spoke of Mme Tussaud's, it was as if she had been personally acquainted with the old lady.

My mother's mother, Vera, despite her German antecedents, did not speak with an accent, nor indeed did she speak a word of any language other than English, but she was a raging xenophile. When anyone from *abroad* came to the house, she would demand that they say something to her in their own language, and when they obliged she went into a sort of ecstatic trance, closing her eyes and swaying back and forth with delight, then demanded that they repeat it all over again. In her front room were portraits of her grandparents, engravings executed by her grandfather (he had come to England to be art master at Marlborough College; Fleuss's arch, still standing, is named after him). Every night before retiring she would drink a toast to them. She was under the deluded impression that they were Habsburgs; in fact they were Rhinelanders from as far back as records existed. But after drinking the toast my grandmother would put on a record of a Johann Strauss waltz and whizz round the room as she had done as a young woman, in double time, her dainty feet somehow maintaining the balance of her considerable bulk.

The time of her life had been the Second World War. London was flooded with émigrés in flight from the Nazis, and my grandmother's personal contribution to the war effort was to fling her doors open to them all. Every weekend and on many weekdays the house would be filled with Polish pilots, Armenian attachés, Free French, German Jews, all required to say something in their own language, sing songs from their homelands, remember their native woods and fields. The beer and the spirits flowed freely and love – and probable death – were in the air. All, of course, long vanished by the time I appeared. But those mad polyglot days were still alive and as emotionally charged as ever for her.

My grandmothers were the rocks on which I built my life, and in my mind they were fundamentally associated with what we then used to call the Continent, a word that still for me evokes a sense of other colours, other possibilities, of a sophistication and a subtler set of values than the ones I felt around me. All this was reinforced by Nic Frizelle, a Frenchman who taught at my grammar school. Nic, who had fought with the Free French during the war, took me under his very Gallic wing and, with no ulterior motive that I could ever discern, would invite me for supper to his place, where he inculcated the mysteries of high French culture into me. We would listen to his LPs of Debussy's *Pélléas et Mélisande*, drink perfectly chilled white wine and discuss Racine and Corneille and the meaning of divine grace. As a present, he gave me a superb annotated edition of Baudelaire's *Les Fleurs du Mal*. Casement after casement opened up onto a culture that I saw – because Nic made me see – that I, as a European, belonged to.

Though my grandmothers embodied in themselves so much that was European, they firmly believed that Britain was Best. Mater wept at the Last Night of the Proms, her magnificent contralto basso belting out 'Land of Hope and Glory', she was passionate about the Boat Race and struggled to her feet for the National Anthem. Toto, on a rare visit to Paris, found it so much less salubrious than London. She never went back to Lyon; Mater, for her part, never went any further afield than the Isle of Wight. And even I, by then passionate about everything European – favouring Italian, French and German films far above anything originating in the United States – had never, at the age of twenty, been to Europe.

It was not until one Sunday in 1968 when a gang of us from various West End box offices went on a day trip to Calais that I finally took that giant step. We made a beeline for a pleasant-looking little restaurant on the beach. Once in the door my nostrils were assailed by unprecedented aromas, bewildering in their variety and intensity.

Salivating like a hound, I sat down to examine the sizeable menu. My grandmothers were both fine cooks, but this was something else. It was like going to the theatre: everything had a flourish, an arrogance about it. Each dish stood up on its hind legs, challenged you, demanded to be eaten, expected applause. I ordered *Tournedos Rossini*, having no idea what it might be, simply because I was a great fan of the composer. Layer after layer – the foie gras, the beef, the gravy-saturated toast – overwhelmed me.

This was a turning point in my life, like making love for the first time; life suddenly had a new meaning. The whole experience was intensely erotic, and intimately bound up with being *abroad*. A year later, now a drama student, I was in Paris, on the Left Bank, in an atticky little hotel room, with my boyfriend; no eyebrows were raised. For Paris, I thought, read Paradise. Since then I have endlessly roamed the Continent, consuming everything it has had to offer me – food, drink, plays, pictures, passion – always intoxicated by its otherness, but always feeling part of it. In America, for all its charms, I feel deracinated, alien. In Europe, even in greater Europe, including Poland, Slovenia, Sweden, I feel our history all around me, our parallel journeys. I feel part of the tapestry, the warp and weft of our common experience. The very distinctiveness of each country, its language, its traditions, its music, are part of my unconscious memory. Each of us different but with a common grounding.

I feel this nowhere else in the world, on no other continent, no other landmass. This is what I come out of, this is what I belong to. It's in my blood, in my bones. The ancient accident of geological upheaval that sundered Britain from continental Europe is just that; we are a many-hued, many-faceted entity: a whole. Political structures and divisions may come and go, but this is who we are. A tiny little sleeve of water between us cannot be allowed to be symbolic. We are as one.

WE MOVE AROUND

Louisa Young

I was conceived in a small hotel across the piazza from Turin Cathedral; lost my virginity under a bridge in Florence; finished my first novel in rooms attached to a tiny church in the Tolfa hills; first went on a motorcycle – a Moto Guzzi – round Lake Bracciano in Lazio, in leopard-skin swimming trunks, pillion to a farm boy called Roberto. Italians would say to little blonde and blue-eyed me, 'Where are you from?' I'd answer, '*Sono Inglese*.' 'Oh good,' they'd say. 'We thought you might be German.' They no longer make that kind of comment. Half a century has passed.

My father was at the university in Perugia in the forties; my sister now lives in the Maremma. Before I was born my family lived for eight years in Rome and I never got over it. Through the sixties and seventies we rented a half-ruined castellated stable by the lake. I learned a lot about milking and irrigation channels, but the rare days when we went to Rome were my dream.

My great-great-great-grandmother Rhalou, on my father's side, was Greek, born in Constantinople. Rhalou met a man from Edinburgh in Malta: his dog yapped at her in a shop; she jumped on the table and he helped her down. Their daughter was the first Zoe in England. His sister married Rhalou's brother, the poet Alexandros Rizos-Rangaviss.

My mother was brought up in Switzerland. Her mother had left St Petersburg in 1907 via Finland, with a string of miniature Fabergé eggs stitched into the hem of her petticoat, and drowned in Lake Geneva aged twenty-nine. My Irish great-grandmother came to England from Dublin; Scottish ancestors went to Ireland. Apparently we're descended from Charlemagne, *Pater Europae,* whose unification of Europe lasted till the Great Schism of 1054, and who was given a little fishing village, name of Venice, as a wedding present. He had four wives (Desiderata, Princess of Lombardy; Hildegarde of the Vinzgau; Fastrada, who was Frankish; and Luitgard, who was Alamannian), many concubines, and eighteen children. Being descended from him is nothing special. All Europeans, but for the most recent arrivals, are descended from every ninth-century person whose children survived. Everyone is descended from Charlemagne. He really *is* the Father of Europe.

My first boyfriend, in London, was Greek. My last boyfriend is Dutch, though he hasn't lived there for fifty years. Half of those he spent in Australia (where my Irish grandfather was born); half in Scotland. Periodically I live at a pal's in the south of Tuscany. She's English, been there for thirty years with her family, building a business, educating, and making wine. My accent is good but my Italian is pretty terrible. '*Sei sempre nel presente, come un buddista,*' a friend said. 'You're always in the present, like a Buddhist.'

I took my daughter to Italy before I even knew she existed. Her father – Ghanaian – lived there for five years.

We move around. It's a fact. It's our nature. Out of desire, fear or necessity. Often, we don't move that far. This is not so much to say how we love Europe. It's just to say, we *are* Europe. We are each other.

PIRATE NATION

Jake Arnott

I'm writing this from St Leonards-on-Sea on the Sussex coast, in a flat overlooking the English Channel where I come to write. I look at it at an angle, westwards, along the curve of Pevensey Bay, all the way to Beachy Head. On a clear day I can see the white cliffs below that brooding headland. Some say the Greeks called this island Albion, meaning 'white land', because of the distinctively chalky outline that is first visible at some of these most navigable crossing points.

Somewhere at a midway point of the bay is Pevensey Castle, whose outer walls are the remnants of a Roman fort, part of the Saxon Shore coastal defences that were constructed to keep out those troublesome pirates who would eventually become the English.

In the third century AD Carausius, an admiral responsible for this defensive system, used it to stage his own Brexit from the centralised Roman rule and set himself up as Emperor of an independent Britain. Something of a would-be populist, he had coins minted with bold slogans that declared him *restitutor Britanniae* ('restorer of Britain'); *genius Britanniae* ('spirit of Britain'); and the acronym *RSR – redeunt Saturnia regna –* meaning 'the reign of Saturn is back', in other words 'the golden age has returned'. Well, his plan to make Britannia great again didn't last. Seven years later he was assassinated by his finance minister and the Empire was restored.

But even after the final collapse of that first European super-state, the system that Pevensey Castle represents seemed to continue be operating. There is much debate about the Anglo-Saxon settlement in Britain; some say that these proto-English were already on the Saxon Shore at this time, employed as part of these defences. All over the Empire, friendly tribal forces known as *foederati* had been used as auxiliary soldiers and allowed resident status. And it seems this tradition was continued by a British ruler who, to fill the gap left by the departed legions, invited Anglo-Saxon mercenaries to help with the defence against marauding Picts and Scots. So the primal identity of the English is as *foederati*, from the root *foedus*, meaning 'treaty' or 'agreement'. And this is where we get the word 'federal' from, a term that strikes terror into many a Brexiteer. Misguided by the myths of our own empire, they imagine that federalism means subjugation, but this was how the English first established themselves and became a force to be reckoned with.

The opposite of *foedus* is, quite simply and literally, 'no deal', and for the British along the coastline I now gaze upon this was to prove disastrous. After the agreement between them broke down, a new group of settlers came to Pevensey Bay. The shore fort, still in occupation, was besieged and, according to the Anglo-Saxon Chronicle of AD 491, a new wave of Saxons 'slew all the inhabitants; there was not even one Briton left'. And so the Kingdom of the South Saxons, or Sussex, where I am writing this, was founded.

Englishness is a migrant identity and the very term 'anglo-saxon' is a multicultural one (which included other ethnic groups such as Jutes and Frisians). England was never an 'indigenous' nation.

There were always new arrivals. Vikings plundered this coastline and, of course, William the Conqueror landed in Pevensey in 1066.

And there's much evidence around here of what might have made the mix had history taken a different turn. The system of fire beacons on the Downs to warn of the Spanish Armada, a Martello tower built on the shoreline to repel Napoleon. But it's misleading to always frame our relationship with Europe in terms of defence and conquest.

In the square below my flat there's a statue of Queen Victoria, staring defiantly out at the English Channel. There's a hole in her skirts made by a stray bullet from a German aircraft during the last great threat to our shores. But let's remember that the Nazis were trying to keep us out of Europe because they wanted it for themselves. There was never any real prospect of an invasion; they were trying to ensure we stayed in isolation. Hitler even offered a separate peace, a Brexit that would have given him free hand on the Continent.

Thankfully that fractured vision of Europe was defeated and a union emerged to keep a greater peace. Free movement based on treaty isn't invasion but a peaceful way of regulating what will happen anyway. Humanity is a migrant species; nothing can stop us moving. And we all came from somewhere else, on the *Empire Windrush* or a Saxon longboat.

So let's all go back to where we came from, shall we? Especially when we claim to talk about 'identity' and 'nationalism'. I want my country back too. I want us to be honest about what it was in the first place.

The Channel is calm today, a bright turquoise diffusing into a sharp blue line where the sea meets the sky. But the horizon isn't a border, you know. It's what joins us.

UNITY BY INCLUSION

Jonathan Meades

1

Along the French–Belgian border in the former killing fields between Sedan and Metz grass grows high and sways with the wind. Rain crushes it, pools form on it. They are not absorbed by the earth. I woke to this on a train when I was fourteen. It was like the steppe, which I had seen only in photographs. Despite ideologies which would fall into desuetude, despite regimes which would perish, despite frontiers which might change overnight this landscape with a single tree on the horizon was a blatant sign of connectedness, of a continuity that stretches from the Moselle to the Don, to the Volga and far beyond.

2

Metz. Verlaine's hometown. He wrote that 'its fortress was no fortress – for its Commandant's weapon was a white flag'. Its railway station was designed during the near half-century of annexation of Alsace-Lorraine after the Franco-Prussian war. It is wholly German: *rundbogenstil,* the round arch idiom, forms no part of France's architectural lexicon. Its employment by Jürgen Kröger was a gesture of imperial pomp and colonial subjugation. Now it is just a stop, a magnificent stop, a long peacetime stop, between cities close to invisible borders: Stuttgart and Verdun, Nancy and Frankfurt.

3

Carnoux en Provence is a small town between Marseille and Cassis whose construction began in the late 1950s when French settlers left Morocco and accelerated in 1962/3 with the arrival from Algeria of the deracinated *pieds noirs*, who had been pusillanimously betrayed by de Gaulle. Resentment against the General was such that eleven attempts were made on his life, but the devil has the best armour-plating. Today it is a late modernist period piece whose history is far from forgotten, but while fifth-generation children may know the words of 'Le pays qui n'existe plus', they will have lives to lead which do not involve looking back to the stolen idyll of *là-bas*.

4

Stralsund has the most thrilling skyline. Five years after the wall had come down it was still in the DDR in all but name. Sumptuous Hansa buildings were crumbling. The old certainties and assurances had gone. Ostalgia had kicked in; choice, especially unaffordable choice, was an FDR con. Nylon shirts and broken Trabis were ubiquitous. The food was terrible. The shops were stripped of goods. The people hanging about desolately chain-smoking super-high-tar Roth Handle had reason to resent Westerners. They were coughing, hawking proof that drip-down is a patronising fantasy. Across the Strelasund lies Rugen: Caspar David Friedrich's cliffs, joyous sodomy in the Weimar years – and Prora, the vast industrial holiday complex designed by Clement Clotz for the KdF, Robert Ley's 'Strength Through Joy' – a lie of Johnsonian proportions. Twenty years ago it was partly squatted, mostly derelict. Now, almost eighty years after it was built, it is at last being turned into holiday homes.

5

During the last century Europe invented the most monstrous polities. More importantly, it also invented the means to quash them. Today the continent is largely *healed*. The chances of it remaining so are jeopardised by boastful expressions of exceptionalism, by refusing to acknowledge that we should find our points of communion and celebrate them rather than scream about our differences.

Jonathan Meades, *Adieu Francis le Belge*, 2015.

AUBERGE

Mark Ellen

For years my wife and I and our two small boys used to stay in a town called Balleroy in Normandy in a little roadside inn. Everything about the place was impossibly charming – the cockerels crowing in their overgrown meadow, the dovecote, the beehives, the baking heat, the swifts in the roofbeams, the rich scent of croissants from the boulangerie next door.

The French couple who ran it conjured up magnificent meals for about a fiver, heaps of *escargots de mer*, lamb roasted with apricots and a chilled rice pudding with a dash of calvados. The boys went fishing once and caught a trout and they pan-fried it as an extra course. They couldn't have made us more welcome.

One summer we took my parents and, dodging the rain, found ourselves in a museum in Bayeux with a section on the Second World War including the guns and uniforms of the British Eighth Parachute Battalion. Forty-seven years earlier my father had dropped from a Dakota on a mission to take the nearby bridge at Caen. Days later he'd been hit by a mortar, shipped back to England and awoke in hospital to find he'd lost his left leg. He'd just turned twenty-four. He'd barely talked about his active service since. But something about that warm and hospitable roadhouse seemed to unlock the door and the memories came tumbling out. They weren't maudlin or particularly emotional, they were detailed, whimsical and fond. '*J'ai perdu ma jambe à la guerre*,' he told our hosts in his stumbling schoolboy French, '*et maintenant je suis revenu pour la trouver!*' At which point the peach brandy came out and limitless drinks were on the house.

It was intensely moving. Who felt more gratitude and affection? Was it them for my old man's sacrifice? Was it us for the magical French culture we so adored?

WILD, BARE AND NEVER VISITED BY THE SUN IN WINTER

William Dalrymple

Dear fellow Europeans,

I know you've found all of us on this unhappy island quite incredibly annoying for some time. At this moment, when we're on the verge of committing a stupid act of catastrophic self-harm, when, after months of tortuous indecision we still can't agree on anything, you probably don't want to hear any more from anyone on our benighted Isle ever again. But just five minutes. That's all I ask. I won't be long. Come close. Sit down if you'd like to. Listen.

Well, first of all, as a Scot I want to say very clearly that it isn't our fault. Don't roll your eyes. I know all divorcees try to blame the other party – but this really isn't. We Scots have always been the most enthusiastic of Europeans, even if we're on the north-western edge of the continent – indeed maybe because we're on the edge and have only the Atlantic to our backs as we gaze towards you, longingly, admiring your culture and your food and your wine and your paintings and your music and your weather. Maybe, above all, your weather.

In truth, we've always seen our continental neighbours as a lifeline, a counterbalance to our other noisy neighbours to the south. It was they who voted for Brexit. Honestly – we didn't.

Sixty-two per cent of us voted Remain. Only thirty-eight per cent of us were lured by the siren calls of the charlatans – those Brexit fantasists who now stand exposed for the snake oil salesmen we always knew them to be. All their rhetoric has proved demonstrably false. We are not taking back control of anything: instead, we are ceding control of everything, and losing our best friends and natural allies in the process.

We saw – long before everyone else around here – how the Brexiteers were like some monstrous suicide cult who were going to take us all down with them – not just economically (although, make no mistake, as in all divorces, this really is going to hurt our pockets, and not just in lawyer's fees). But it's not just about money. It's not even mainly about the money. It's about much more than that. It's about who we are – where we come from, what we believe in. It's about who our real friends are, who we can trust. Who we love.

Try to understand what this feels like for us.

We've just been forced into a divorce when we're still in love. And in truth, we always loved you. We know already how much we're going to miss you, more keenly with every day that the separation and divorce draws nearer. We know that soon we'll be in the wrong lane at immigration, when we try to fly into Rome or Paris or Lisbon or Leiden or Utrecht – towns where we've spent so much time, over so many centuries. We know we won't find it so easy to do business or to buy a flat near you or even to come on holiday. We may not get a visa to visit you. You may not get a visa to visit us.

Let me speak for myself. I grew up in the Borders during the seventies, constantly surprised how even in the wildest moorlands, links with distant parts of Europe seemed to lie under every clod of soil. As a teenage would-be archaeologist, I used to drive to a field near Melrose and wander over the berms and earthworks of the site of the Roman fortress of Trimontium – named after the three peaks of the Eildon Hills rising above.

In Edinburgh, in the old Museum of Antiquities in Queen Street, I vividly remember when they put on display the astonishing silver masks of the cavalry officers that the archaeologists had dug up there. In one, the face was completely intact. There was something deeply hypnotic about the silent stare of those sad, uncertain, but still handsome Latin faces, from Tuscany perhaps, or maybe the coast near Pompeii, caught forever in their early thirties. Their fleeting expressions were frozen in silver, mouths forever open, startled, as if suddenly surprised by death itself. Their huge, vacant eyes stared out with all the nakedness of a departed soul.

I remember peering through the glass at them, trying to catch some hint of the upheavals they must have witnessed and the strange sights these southern Europeans saw in first-century Scotland – what they made of the Votadini of Traprain Law or our proto-Pictish ancestors, among whose fortresses was one that now lies under Castle Rock. The smooth, silver-gleaming neo-classical faces stared me down. But I learned that you never knew where you might run into the oldest ghosts of continental European culture haunting the most surprising and remote parts of Scotland.

One Easter holiday, my parents took me to Galloway where they hired a cottage near Castle Douglas. There, in a small eighteenth-century chapel, in a remote one-street village in south-west Scotland, I saw one of the most remarkable pieces of Early Christian art to survive anywhere in the British Isles. The

Ruthwell Cross, which dates from the early eighth century and stands some five metres tall, is a fantastically elegant, sophisticated and intricate creation. On the side of the cross is the Eucharistic vinescroll, full of plump Mediterranean grapes, symbolic both of the sacrifice of the Mass and of the Tree of Life. On one face were swirls of carpet-like interlace, whose intricate knots, perhaps copied from a Roman floor mosaic, may have been used then as a sort of talisman to keep the devil at bay.

Nearby, there was an image of the Gospel story of the Healing of the Man Born Blind, representing the opening of the eyes of the heathen. Nearby it was a panel showing Mary Magdalen washing the feet of Christ, a symbol of conversion and repentance. In it, Christ is wearing a toga. It's a Roman image, sculpted by an inhabitant of Scotland, who over one thousand years ago had been given a portable Italian mosaic or icon to copy. I remember being taken to see the cross and descending the circular stairs into the pit where its kept, and being astonished by its sophisticated, classical beauty. Who had made these images, and wrote the extraordinary poem, the *Dream of the Rood*, that covered one face? What was this exotic Romano-Byzantine masterpiece doing in the middle of sleepy rural Galloway?

Nor was it just a one-way traffic. The Celtic monks of Iona received a visit from a Gaulish traveller named Arculf, who told them of his visits to the Holy Places of Palestine. As a teenager on my first visit to Italy, I was astonished to find a very Scottish, Celtic-looking reliquary sitting in the monastery of San Salvatore on the slopes of Mount Amiata in Tuscany, left by some ninth-century Scottish pilgrims heading along the Via Francigena on their way to Rome.

I soon learned of just how early many learned Scots made

their careers in the warm South. My favourite were the tales I had heard of another young Borderer, Michael Scott the Wizard, also from Melrose, who in the thirteenth century ended up travelling from the Borders to Paris and hence to Rome, where he briefly became tutor to the Pope. After a long stay at Palermo, he went on to Toledo, where he acquired a sophisticated knowledge of Arabic. He began to dress in Arab clothes and developed a passion for Eastern literature – which was probably the beginning of his reputation as a wizard. His language skills opened up to him the Arabic versions of Aristotle, and also brought him into contact with original works by Avicenna and Averroes. In time he became one of the savants whom the Holy Roman Emperor, Frederick II, *Stupor Mundi* – Wonder of the World – attracted to his brilliant court. As well as mathematics and medicine, Scott had a deep interest in the occult, alchemy, astrology and sorcery.

His reputation for prophecy eventually led to Scott being appointed by Frederick as court astrologer, where he successfully predicted the outcome of a war with the North Italian Lombard League. Scott's dark magic even enabled him to foresee his own death, which he believed would be caused by a stone falling on his head. As a precaution, he wore an iron helmet at all times. But, at least according to Border folklore, he took it off while taking Mass in Melrose and, as predicted, a small stone did indeed fall on his head, causing his death in 1235. He is the only Scot to appear in Dante's *Inferno*, where his reputation as a necromancer won him a posthumous place in the Eighth Circle of Hell, enduring horrific tortures in the company of other distinguished sorcerers, magi and enchantresses.

As with any relationship, not all contacts were happy, of

course. When Aeneas Piccollomini of Pienza was made Pope Pius II, he failed to launch the last Crusade that he spent much of his life planning. This was because he died prematurely of the chilblains he caught making an ill-advised, barefoot winter pilgrimage from Dunbar to the shrine of Our Lady in Whitekirk, through an East Lothian landscape he described in his memoirs as 'wild, bare and never visited by the sun in winter.' Pintorricchio made an extraordinary painting of this Scottish journey that still hangs in the Piccollomini Chapel in Siena Cathedral.

Throughout the Middle Ages, Scots allied with Europeans against our troublesome southern neighbours. The Auld Alliance led us into close political union with the French court, including a succession of marriage alliances with European grandees such as Mary of Guise, who brought over, direct from the continent, waves of European architects, painters and musicians to beautify our buildings and act like leaven to our arts and literature.

These European links lasted long after the Auld Alliance lapsed at the Union, and long after Bonnie Prince Charlie, himself descended from the Medici, retired to drink himself to death in his Florentine Palazzo. Scottish castles were built with pointed turrets, like witches' hats, modelled on those of the Loire, and Scottish domestic houses had crows-step gables based on those in the Hague and Amsterdam. The red pantiles that roofed the steadings of East Lothian first came over as ballast from Rotterdam. Alan Ramsay learned his skills in portraiture in Naples. When Robert Adam returned from the Grand Tour, he reinvented the architecture of the whole island with ideas taken from the sketches he made as a boy from the Palladian palaces of Italy and from amidst the ruins of Pompeii and Herculaneum and the palace of Diocletian in Split. Colen Campbell of

Cawdor's architectural ideas, also brought back from his Italian travels, were the basis for the architecture of the new city of St Petersburg.

Continental European tastes permeated every aspect of Scottish life. We drank claret from vineyards that Scottish vintners bought up in the Bordeaux, and port which Scottish families such as the Cockburns and the Sandemans made from their estates in the Portuguese Douro. When our scholars wished to undertake further studies, they left their books in Edinburgh and St Andrews not for Oxford but for Paris and Utrecht: from 1572 to 1800, 1460 Scots students enrolled in the University of Leiden.

So when the Little Britain Brexiteers tell us now that our future lies with them, and that we must turn our backs on Europe, I feel not just angry but also understand that this diktat goes against all that we are, and all that has formed us. It is not just an act of economic and political suicide, it is an act of massive cultural and philosophical vandalism. How did we allow this to happen? How do we begin to unravel this mess? How badly have we failed both our forefathers and our children?

This came home to me most bitterly last year, when I saw Angela Merkel and Emmanuel Macron arm in arm on Remembrance Day. They both braved the wind and rain, in a way that President Trump refused to do, to remember all our dead, and to learn the lesson that we must all come together to make sure it never happens again. I understood then the scale of what had been achieved in the last sixty years by a continent which had torn itself apart so often, and I realised then more clearly than ever who our real friends are – and the bleak, utter foolishness of separating ourselves from them.

IF MUSIC BE THE
FOOD OF LOVE

LIGHT AND HEAVY

Pete Townshend

In the early days of the sixties the Beatles larked about like American-style, suit-wearing, wise-cracking comedians. When British pop music started, it was playing about with American styles: rhythm and blues, of course, but also *light entertainment.*

Something about pop music then seemed at odds with my youthful anxiety, the inner turmoil welling up inside me – and many others in my generation.

In the mid-sixties, one of my closest and most important friends, and my musical mentor, was Kit Lambert, son of Constant Lambert, musical director of the Royal Opera House, Covent Garden (and model for Hugh Moreland in Anthony Powell's *Dance to the Music of Time*). Kit was allowed to use his mother's permanent box, and when he wasn't using it, I did. The ushers got to know me. I didn't even have to dress up. If I was passing Covent Garden I simply walked in and took my place, often nodding at salubrious old Lord Goodman in the adjacent box.

I came from a musical family – my mother sang very well, and my father played saxophone and clarinet in a big band – and I'd been to classical concerts before at the Royal Albert Hall, but I think it was the immersive experience of opera that began an inner transformation that led to a creative breakthrough.

I can vividly remember entering the warm, plush, soft, deeply red interior of the opera house for the first time. It had an anatomical quality, a sensuality about it, almost a sleaze, like Dali's Mae West lips. If there had been something staid and Sunday-best about a classical concert, the experience of going to the opera was wild, excessive and sensual, giving expression to the fiercest and sometimes most forbidden desires. The fantastical plots pleased me, too, and the mythical images sank deep.

Since early childhood I'd been hearing complex and inspiring orchestral sounds, weird anomalous sounds like nothing in the real world. Some seemed an expression of the desire to escape the drab life of a young West London boy in what were the grey post-war years of the fifties. Others were ethereal. I heard this music first at about seven years old, playing repetitive chords on my Aunt Trilby's out-of-tune piano. A few years later, on a boat trip on the Thames with other schoolboys, I began to hear sounds increasing in complexity until they sounded like an angelic choir. (My friend Ted Hughes later told me he thought I'd heard the music of the spheres.)

Once we were ashore, I kept asking the others if they'd heard the sounds, but none had. I feared I was going mad.

Later I would yearn to recapture those sounds and the rich complex harmonic beauty that I believed was somehow locked away inside them, but it seemed futile.

Now listening to the strange unresolved chords of Wagner and the dissonances of Berg, I began to imagine how I might process the aural hallucinations I was hearing, or even describe them, compose them, or commission an orchestral composer to help me musicalise them. (This a process I have dramatised in my novel The Age of Anxiety, also conceived as a rock opera.)

It was because of very European influences, then, these weird and twisted outgrowths of European high culture, absorbed in the plush surroundings of the Royal Box, that The Who shed its *Top of the Pops* trappings and became the 'Orrible 'Oo. The deep and often dark European past jived with the more recent American era of joyful and restorative pop, blues and theatre musical.

This was the late sixties and it was the time that rock got heavy.

EUROPE ENDLESS EUROPE

Paul Morley

Music took me to Europe. Before I travelled to Europe for the first time at twenty, my northern family never venturing beyond cheap seaside England for our annual holidays, there was the sound of Europe, extra exotic and tantalising because it came from unknown places I only came across abstractly through selective television or dry history lessons. Learning – or not learning – French at school did not give me Europe, but music did. Even the bouncy kitsch and national eccentricities of the sixties and seventies Eurovision Song Contest created a certain emotional connection to a crazy idea of togetherness, but Europe mostly came to me through music that had an experimental, speculative, space-age quality.

In the late sixties a new generation of German musicians influenced intellectually by avant-garde classical music and psychedelic rock started using electronics to make music, generating their own version of a brave new post-war world: peaceful, if noisy; optimistic, if disorientating. By using electronics as a surrealist tool, a futurist lever, taking orbital flights into sound, they were also instantly remaking and remixing rock and pop music, fantastically subverting its brand-new traditions.

Throughout the rest of pop music's history, alongside the obvious foundational American energies and the impertinent, artful British twists, there was always the modernist, post-modernist

European pulse, an exploratory European aura represented by border-dissolving future sounds, different sensations, hidden histories. The electronics that emerged from the austere laboratories and workshops of France and Germany in the fifties travelled into dub, hip hop, house and beyond; ethereal, radical Europe positively influencing black music, white music. Not just taking from liberating black originality but now giving back new possibilities, fractured rhythms and undiscovered spaces.

Perhaps it was listening in the early seventies to Can, Faust, Neu!, Cluster, Popol Vuh – their names alone transmitting the language of Europe – that meant that when I voted for the first time it was to say 'Yes' to Europe in the 1975 referendum. It seemed obvious that you would want to belong to something that directly connected you with these mysterious, seductive sounds and signals. Music then physically took me to Europe as a twenty-year-old music writer interviewing bands on tour in Spain, France, Germany, Holland, Denmark; the architecture, roads, scenery, voices, atmosphere providing overlapping differences and similarities that made captivating sense to me, having been prepared for it by music.

The Europe that sound had placed in my mind was perfectly reflected by the great techno-romantics Kraftwerk as I began my own European visits in 1977. Kraftwerk heralded the re-emergence of a distinct German culture embedded within an overall utopian sense of collective European progress and did it as a 'pop group', enigmatic classical artists producing pop music. They didn't lose their local or national identity – quite the contrary. They gained something else.

The group's *Trans-Europe Express* album began its sonic railway excursion through an imaginary shape-shifting Europe with the poetically constant nine minutes of 'Europe Endless'. A dream European Union anthem, an exquisite soundtrack to freedom of movement, a moving celebration of civilisation, it was a love song to Europe but also a lament, for how vulnerable it was, darkness forever circling.

The music glides ever forward through history, landscape, cities, sadness, people, beauty, day, night, trauma, tension, loneliness, pleasure and music – the curious, questing music of an otherworldly Europe from Mozart to Webern, Brahms to Varese, Schubert to Stockhausen, Debussy to Tangerine Dream, Bach to Kraftwerk. It portrays a never changing ever-changing Europe, as timeless continent and coalescing concept, always reforming and remaking itself after the bloodiest – and stupidest – forms of damage and disruption.

You can leave it, hate it, insult it, reject it, challenge it, destroy it, but you cannot stop it, because Europe, as pure place, as elaborate invention, as Kraftwerk sublimely divined, never ends.

POLYPHONY

Richard Mabey

We had gone to Corsica in Easter week for the flowers. We could smell the *maquis* before we were even walking in it, a warm and resinous scent of lavender, myrtle, thyme, juniper. This is the vegetation that helps define the Mediterranean, a suite of shrubs that grow from the Baltic and the Middle East to Iberia and back again along the north African coast, always changing in height and structure, but united in their aromatic tanginess. This is the south – vivid, cosmopolitan, open-faced, with a warmth that flows, when it is permitted, to the north.

This proved to be the character of the local music, too. We were staying in the coastal town of Calvi. From our hotel room we could see Europe's two geographical extremes. Dolphins leaped in the kingfisher-blue sea, just as they leaped in a Knossos mural dated to 1600 BC. Just to the east we could see the snow-capped peak of Monte Cinto, where we'd later find shoals of the miniature crocuses we grew at home – another reminder of how southern Europe has enriched the north. The day before Good Friday we were exploring the area round the Citadel, when we heard, from somewhere nearby, the sound of male singing voices. We tracked them to the Oratoire St-Antoine, where we found a group of men (we recognised some of the waiters from the hotel) rehearsing Corsica's indigenous music, *polyphonie corse*. It was not quite like any music I had heard before, but then again seemed full of poignant echoes. There was the sound of northern Europe plainsong, of Hebrew chants and Moorish quartertone cadences, of Roma and klezmer melodies. It was ornate but intensely focused, the singers standing in a circle, eyes closed, one hand cupped over the ear, resolving expansive chords into momentary dissonance. In the forties, the great scholar of Corsica Dorothy Carrington wrote that polyphony was like 'a song from a beginning that one never dares believe is possible'. The next day we saw the group perform on Calvi's great Good Friday procession of penitents, waiters' striped trousers just visible under their hooded cassocks.

We heard more polyphony in the days that followed, and found out a little of its history, how it was the basis of both the secular folk music of the mountains and the *maquis,* and of the island's religious celebrations. In the twentieth century it had almost died out, but went through a dramatic revival during the struggle for Corsican independence in the seventies. Now it thrives in many kinds of world music hybrids.

Polyphony is uniquely Corsican, but its popular roots and its borrowing from many musical cultures recur across the Mediterranean. I've heard echoes of it in a Fado bar in Lisbon, where talking was forbidden during singing, and where the waiters were again performers, their whole physiques transformed by the discipline of singing. And in a hut in the wilds of Extremadura, where four gipsy forest workers gave an electrifying display of unaccompanied flamenco during their lunch break.

The composer Osvaldo Golijov wrote his homage to Europe's cultural diversity, *Ayre* (2004), around such musics. In his accompanying notes he suggests: 'With a little bend, a melody goes from Jewish to Arab to Christian. How connected these cultures are and how terrible it is when they don't understand each other. The grief that we are living in the world today has already happened for centuries, but somehow harmony *was* possible between these civilisations.'

MUSIC, A SHARED FRIENDSHIP

Evelyn Glennie

I'm thinking how I have seen almost the entire width and breadth of Europe, whether travelling by plane or by truck, transporting my myriad of percussion instruments miles upon miles from country to country within the EU. On my travels I have met, performed and dined with amazing people of all ages and backgrounds. I have made many friends and enjoyed a great deal of companionship with the citizens of the countries that currently form the European Union.

In my experience, music creates a bond between people and countries, and those bonds are not easily broken by rules or regulations, politics or congress.

I have witnessed the disappearance of walls and softening of borders, thus making way for the ease of travel and immense freedom to move through landscapes that have inspired artists whose genius bedecks the galleries of the world. Most of all I have benefitted from the kindness of my fellow European citizens who have shared in my passion for music and sound.

Whilst times are changing, one thing I am certain of is that music continues to bind us. It's a glue that spans country to country, stage to stage and note to note. Music ignites curiosity and conversation, patience and responsibilities, ownership and shared experiences. Music creates bridges and I am determined to help create more bridges through the art of listening to each other and to our environment. Through listening we create the landscape for building memories – priceless treasures that will remain in our hearts forever.

WHEN BLACKBIRDS SING

Mark Cocker

A European blackbird has taken up residence in our October garden, a scruffy half-moulted creature with feathers still missing from its rounded head. Yet the beak is already an adult male's yellow-orange and in March I know it will open again and out will pour that fruit-filled, sunshine music of meditative phrases that are the quintessence of its species' song. The author W. H. Hudson thought it the bird vocalisation closest to human utterance. I think of it as a sort of beautiful avian oratory.

As in every spring in my life when I first hear the insinuating softness of it, I will be reminded of other occasions when blackbirds have sung. And not just here, but all across its range, for blackbirds are common from the Urals to the Atlantic shores of Ireland or Spain. A telling aspect of that European distribution is that blackbirds love to be near us. They achieve their highest breeding numbers and success, not in the pristine forest where they originated, but in suburbia. We would not be entirely wrong to imagine that they like to sing to us.

I remember especially one Greek blackbird singing to me in a place I know called Dilofo, a silent Epirot village among the Pindos mountains in a region called Zaghori. Somewhere lost in foliage so dense it felt subaquatic, the bird soloed above a distant barking dog and it seemed a distillation of all the chlorophyll in that green, wet, dawn Spring wood.

Another occasion I recall distinctly was at the bottom of a steep valley near the small town of Colmenar in Andalucía, in the hills behind – and a world away – from the razzmatazz of the Costa del Sol. Golden orioles and bee-eaters were overhead, but the sound I retain best is the late-afternoon chorus of several blackbirds. It rose from the gorge, where self-sown oleanders filled the floor with shade and Iberian water frogs clustered in a pocket of damp shadow on the bank where a spring burst from its aged, manmade cave. The song of all those unseen blackbirds blended to a sort of chaotic harmony that was loamy and fertile, but also deeply familiar amid all that dazzling Moorish sunshine.

There is something else entailed in blackbird song that I cherish. Wherever and whenever we hear this bird of home there is infused with the intrinsic pleasure of its sound a further kind of comfort: an exquisite sense of commonality flowing from the fact that all this continent is, in a sense, one united empire held under the swaying song of blackbirds.

Almost simultaneously, with some adjustment for the declination of the sun according to latitude or longitude – maybe outside the bars in Barcelona and Berlin, or in the avenues of Belgrade, perhaps in Athens or Kalambaka; but also for the folk at post-work drinks in Bangor or Basingstoke, Brora and Beauly – blackbirds will be singing to us all on any spring evening.

None of us can escape – even should we wish to – this collective song of Europe. It is a part of our common heritage that infuses and shapes our ecosystem. It is embedded in our shared consciousness. It is a portion of a precious birthright granted to us all.

ANGOISSE DES GARES

A FAREWELL TO EUROPE

Colin Tudge

Europe is not the only great civilisation and I do not want to suggest that it is the greatest. China, India, Arabia, Turkey, Nigeria, Mexico and many more – all have given rise to great civilisations and all have brought wondrous things to the world. The history of Europe is largely unspeakable and it is still deeply flawed. Of course, too, Europe is hugely heterogeneous, pulling this way and that, and whatever is good is often outweighed by what is all too obviously vile. The Ancient Greeks, who invented democracy (or at least invented the word) and laid the foundations of Western art, philosophy and much of science, and are presented in our most ancient and venerated schools as paragons, were also wondrous cruel.

But Europe certainly has the ingredients of greatness. Chauvinism is a dreadful and destructive thing, yet I feel, chauvinistically, that with due care, Europe more than most could still provide a model for the whole world, showing how life could be both for us and for our fellow creatures – not just for the next few desperate decades but for many centuries to come. At the very least, if it is humanity's ambition truly to create a better world, kinder and more secure and ever more diverse, then Europe with its cross-the-board ingenuity and underlying morality and metaphysics, must be a key player.

England is my home and I will defend it like family. I was born here and have always lived here and know no other languages apart from *cerveza* and *Danke schön*. Often, though, when we're in France or Italy or wherever, I feel that Europe's assessment of Albion through most of history has been perfectly justified. We *are* barbarian. So we have conserved our stately homes where the very rich live, but we have largely wrecked the cities and villages of past centuries that were home to the rest of us. We have nothing comparable to, say, Bruges. We never did of course – not quite like that. But we did have a great deal else that should have been treasured, and yet, more zealously than any other Western European country it seems, we let the planners loose on it. And, of course, the speculators.

More generally, it seems to me, the countries of mainland Europe follow as a matter of course, and without usually thinking about it, the core teaching of St Benedict. That is, they focus much more than we do on the minutiae of everyday life – the details that are the stuff of good living and civilisation, a firm base for conviviality and for loftier flights. Architecture is one example of this. Food, very strikingly, is another. Civilisations can and must be built around food – both the cooking and the raising of it. In particular, all the world's greatest cuisines from Italy to China use meat very sparingly – as stock or garnish and for only occasional feasts – and make best use of whatever grows locally. If everyone everywhere learned to cook like the world's best cooks (not the celebrity chefs – just the many millions who cook for their families) and farmed accordingly (small organic farms with not many animals and lots of tender loving care) then everyone in the world could be well fed, to the very highest standards.

So it is that while Britain has Sainsbury's and Wetherspoons and KFC and Travelodge, Belgium, France, Italy, Germany, Holland, and Switzerland still have a host of wondrous patisseries and charcuteries and family-run cafes and *auberges,* still serving wondrous dishes that often are unique to themselves. One of the most memorable meals I ever had, with my wife, was in Siena – of tripe, cow's intestines: beautifully marinated and herbed with local tomatoes and garlic and white beans, and a very ordinary but very drinkable local wine. We could all live like that, but Britain, apparently, has chosen not to. Tripe, insofar as it is obtainable at all, is traditionally served in big white slabs, seethed in milk, with onions. Not appetizing. Yet all it needs is a little technique – and of course a little focus on the minutiae of life, on which the rest can be built.

There is much that's ghastly and getting worse on mainland Europe, but on the whole they seem to hang on to *values* – historical, moral, metaphysical – far better than we are doing. Nowhere else in the world apart from the US, to whose coat-tails we are encouraged to cling, has embraced neoliberalism as zealously as successive British governments have done. None other is quite so committed to short-term wealth at the expense of everything else. Most – all? – European countries of sufficient power have a grisly imperial past but none hang on to it quite as sedulously or proudly as Britain does, or choose to imagine, as Britain does, that it is still a world power that should 'take back control' and 'go it alone'; or imagines that this is a worthy ambition.

I feel, vicariously, somewhat irrationally, and no doubt presumptuously, as an ordinary human being on the edge of Europe, an affinity with the European greats. I feel in a very odd way that St Francis, Schubert, the French Impressionists, Einstein,

Erasmus, Dante (not that I've ever read any Dante) are my family. They certainly featured large in my education if only, in some cases, by name. In short, I feel that Europe is a club that I want to belong to, and felt, when we were part of the EU, that I did belong to. Brexit is a bereavement, a perversely self-inflicted banishment; and in all literature, banishment is seen as the most grievous of punishments. Britain's secession brings Matthew Arnold's *Dover Beach* to mind: a 'melancholy, long, withdrawing roar' leaving in its wake the 'naked shingles of the world'.

Welcome to the world of naked shingles and bilateral trade agreements.

JE T'AIMAIS, JE T'AIME ET JE T'AIMERAI

Cathy Rentzenbrink

In 1994 I spent a few months living in Normandy, in a seaside town called Courseulles sur Mer which bore many marks of its wartime history. My tiny studio flat was on Avenue de la Combattante; I was just around the corner from Avenue de La Libération and only a few hundred metres from one of the beaches that had seen the troops disembark on D-Day, fifty years earlier.

I was nineteen and had always dreamed of living in France, but was lost in sadness because my brother was very ill and I was slowly and painfully coming to understand that he would never get better. I spent a lot of time walking around war cemeteries thinking about damage and death, and humming a song by Francis Cabrel, '*Je t'aimais, je t'aime et je t'aimerai.*' I loved you, I love you and I will love you. For me it captured, still does, something essential about the nature of grief and longing.

It was a privilege that I didn't fully appreciate at the time to be right in the heart of the fiftieth anniversary of D-Day celebrations. I was there as the *anciens combattants* descended en masse; sweet, doddery, grey-haired men who at my age had stormed the beaches, been shot at, watched their comrades die, and then gone home to grow old. I watched as they walked around memory lane with misty eyes, pointing to familiar sights with liver-spotted hands.

The war seemed far away to me then, safely entombed in the past. These days I feel it getting closer. I keep rereading Second World War novels. It makes me nervous to read how people laughed at Hitler and dismissed him as no threat, and how quickly cordial relations between nations disintegrated into war. Is it excessively melodramatic to draw parallels with how we live now? I do hope so.

In 2024 it will be the eightieth anniversary of D-Day. It's unlikely there will be many *anciens combattants* around to mark it. Will the UK really not be part of the European Union by then? I still don't understand how we arrived at this point. I sometimes wonder if I'm trapped in a long and meandering nightmare from which I might wake up. 'I had this strange dream,' I will say to my Dutch husband. 'Donald Trump was president of the USA and we were leaving the European Union. You'd been rebranded an "EU National" and Nigel Farage was always on the telly. None of our politicians gave the slightest shit about Northern Ireland and Boris Johnson was Prime Minister!'

It is a nightmare, but I don't think it's possible to wake up. All I can do is weep. It does feel a bit like grief, this huge sadness. I flicker between anger and denial and depression and am a long way from any kind of acceptance. I don't accept it. I refuse this exit. I'm still hoping something will be done, that sanity will reassert itself. When our politicians talk about what British people want, I boil with rage. When they talk disrespectfully about Europe and about Europeans, I flood with shame.

Europe, you see me before you, confused and impotent, lost and sad. I can only apologise and send words of love. *Je suis desolée.* I'm sorry. *Je t'aimais, je t'aime et je t'aimerai.* I loved you, I love you and I will love you.

LOVE, MIGRATION AND IMAGINING THE FUTURE, WITH HOPE

Jackie Morris

As a child it was hard to imagine what this thing called Europe was that people spoke of. My world was a garden, where small birds came and went. Later at school I saw maps, the shape of the land, a globe. How tiny 'Great Britain' seemed when viewed on this globe. How minute it was, when those images came back from space of the sun rising over the globe, blue and green and turning in an ocean of the universe.

In Britain we live in a collection of countries that can be driven across in a day. As a child, though, I never went far from home. The longest journey I did was through Worcestershire, Gloucestershire and Somerset to Devon, passing the borders of counties, landmarks that made the blood race and spoke of 'holidays'.

I grew up loving the shape of birds, learning their names, their migrations, the pathways in the sky they followed to the lands and seas I saw on those coloured maps of the world. And I learned that these shapes and colours marked the borders of countries. It came as a shock to learn that as humans we required a thing called a passport to cross these borders. I began to learn that the land I lived in was 'owned' by certain people, finding it hard to understand. How could humans own a tree that was growing before they were born and would live on after they had died? How could people own land that was shared with so many species? I looked to the sky. Always a dreamer.

And then came the biggest blow. I was drawing, nose to the sketchbook. The television was on. Black and white. It was the *World at War*. The episode about the Holocaust. I watched, appalled. Something inside me broke.

And then I learned of this gathering of countries, the European Union, that grew out of the ashes of war. A linking of people for social justice, a European Court to champion human rights. Despite my newfound knowledge of the grievous deeds we are capable of, I thought to myself: maybe there is hope in this world.

To me, Europe is not a landmass. Just as Great Britain is not a collection of countries. Both are human constructs, ideas shaped from a desire to 'own'. And yet there are so many other species in this world, creatures of the sky and the earth, of rivers and forests. Why are we so covetous?

Europe is a coming together of people, and being a part of Europe, being integrated in that union, is personal for me.

Imagine, if you can, a small child, maybe twelve or thirteen. She's standing at a dockside with a suitcase in hand. She's excited. She's going to school in another country. For weeks now she's sat on the swing that hangs from the doorway inside the apartment they call home, gently swinging and watching the light reflected on the ceiling, fractured patterns reflected from water in the canal below, listening to her parents talk of visas and sponsors. She has her one precious book of birds, and she knows how to speak English and she's travelling with a teacher from the school. She hugs her mother goodbye and wishes she would stop making such a fuss and kisses her father on the cheek.

Across the sea, a new land, a new school. And she can't

understand what these people say as they speak so fast. But she learns. And she reads her bird book and sees here familiar birds that remind her of home.

Letters from home come, for a while, then they stop. She doesn't know why. She is lonely. The school moves, away from the coast, where bombs are beginning to fall, but they leave her behind. Fourteen years old by now and she's growing out of her clothes. She has no money, and even if she did have it, she doesn't know how to buy clothes, where from. She's always hungry, surviving on buns from a bakery. On a good day they have currants in them. Now every day she goes to the Jewish Refugee Centre, where at least she feels safe. Here she sits and cries . . . and waits. They can't help her. She has no paperwork, no one to speak for her. Then one day the military police come. They take away all the men who work there. She sees a chance, and offers to work. Now, at least, she has money.

Later she learns why the letters from her parents stopped.

Later she marries, has two children. One of them I met and fell deeply in love with. He lives because at one time his mother had the right piece of paper to cross a border. He never knew his grandparents, because they didn't.

When Lottie died, among her papers were things called 'alien cards'. There were letters of heartbreak from a detective she had employed to seek out the truth of what had happened to her parents. Three calm, kind, matter-of-fact, handwritten letters on light, lined paper explaining that there was no sign of them at the apartment she had lived in, nor any knowledge from neighbours as to their whereabouts. The trail led to a ghetto where all the Jews from that area had been taken. There were two survivors: neither were Lottie's parents. The kindness in the phrase in the letter 'I can assure you they did not suffer' is an unbearable lie. My memory carries a vision of the ghost of the child, swinging in the doorway, watching the light.

Europe is a human concept. Its power lies in togetherness. We face a time of great challenge now that goes beyond mere humans. Setting up more borders and divisions only makes a mockery of the task we have at hand: to imagine a new way for humans to live on this earth together not just with each other, but with ALL life on earth. Only together can we do this, with imagination, courage and hopeful hearts.

Also among Lottie's things is a small book called *Birds of Britain*. Carried across a continent, spine broken, cover loose, as a talisman from home. Birds know no borders. Why should we?

NOT SOMEONE LIKE YOU

Michel Faber

'Oh, it won't come to that, surely?' This is a phrase I've heard
many times in the last three years. It's uttered by friendly,
cultured, open-minded people in my town – the sort of people
who woke up on the morning of 24 June 2016 blinking in disbelief
at finding their values outvoted. Since that day, they've reassured
themselves that the fracture in our society can be reversed, as if a
pane of glass can be talked out of the crack in it, as if a burst
balloon can be made to see that staying intact is the best thing all
round.

I tell them that Brexit reclassifies me an illegal alien, officially
Unsettled, unless I apply to Britain's xenophobic government for
permission to stay. 'But you're British, surely?' No, I am not
British. 'But you've lived here for so long.' Yes, but that's not the
point. This whole business is about rejecting multiculturalism,
sorting out who's Us and who's Them. I am not Us. 'Well, can't
you just apply?' Of course I can apply. But I don't want to. It's
wrong. It stinks. 'You've got nothing to worry about, surely? I
mean, come on, they're not going to send police to your flat to
deport you. Not someone like you.' I don't know what to say to
these soft-hearted British Europhiles with their quaint notions
of where the march of history will be too principled to go, their
feeling that a Dutchman who speaks English ever so well and

wrote a book as fab as *The Crimson Petal and the White* would surely be exempted from government regulations.

I wonder where I'll go, if I have to leave. The obvious place is the Netherlands, where I was born. But I remember almost nothing from the first seven years of my life. They were spent in Den Haag, apparently, but Den Haag to me is just a railway station. If you deposit me outside a certain hotel whose name I've blanked on just now, I can probably find my way to a certain record shop, if it hasn't gone bust since I was last there.

Two decades ago, when *Onderhuids*, the Dutch translation of *Under the Skin*, was about to be published and I travelled to Holland to help promote it, a local journalist drove me to the neighbourhood where I spent my early years. He was intrigued by what I'd said in interviews about childhood trauma, the factors that led my parents to cut themselves off from their other children and emigrate with me to Australia, the frighteningly blank spaces in my memory where most people have formative stories. He was convinced that if he took me to the place where I'd lived, parked me in the street where I'd played, something would come back to me. We sat in the car for a while, with the tape recorder running. I thanked him for his kindness. Then we returned to the hotel, and I packed my bag for the airport.

A love letter to Europe? I already wrote it, twenty-six years ago, to Britain, and I thought the answer was yes.

OVER THERE

Peter J. Conradi

At sixteen I started hitch-hiking all over Europe. One trip in particular made a big impact. During the bitter winter of 1962 I hitched lifts from London to Berlin to watch the new Wall open temporarily that Christmas. Families divided in the different post-war zones came all too briefly together again. There were many tears. There was much embracing. I no longer recall why this relaxation of formalities was permitted. A stooped old widow in black collected kindling in the freezing fog near the Wall and declined to talk, muttering fearfully '*Ich spreche keine Politik*'. Despite heavy snowfall, war devastation was still visible. Shady characters in the Eastern sector accosted you, seeking illegal currency deals. The Berliner Ensemble was open for business but I had no money to attend. '*Kommst du von da drüben?*', a stranger asked, a question pregnant with envy and a deep yearning for freedom, not least the freedom to travel. 'Do you come from over there?'

Many years later, in 1989, the fall of the Wall was the most thrilling, healing and brilliant event; still now hard to believe. Soon the British Council, to my delight, offered to send me for two years to live in Krakow, Poland, to teach English literature at the Jagiellonian University. I proudly learned some Polish – not an easy language; then I watched with fascination as this gallant country struggled to regain its liberty. In one week it was said that 30,000 Russian school-teachers – in a classically Polish and therefore dramatic gesture – were sacked. But those teachers who also knew English could hope to be re-employed quickly as so few people spoke it at that time. There was still very little in the shops, which gave rise to all sorts of jokes about scarcity.

'Do you have eggs for sale?'

'No. We're the shop that doesn't have vegetables. The shop that doesn't have eggs is round the corner.'

Access to food was helped if you had a country cousin with a smallholding.

Travel to the UK was vexed and I watched Poles stand for four hours in the ice and snow in Warsaw, waiting patiently to apply for visas. Poland's accession to the EU was moving and joyous. Perhaps Europe would be nearly whole again.

On the day of the Brexit vote in 2016 I was on meditation retreat in the Limousin, in France. Six of the sixty retreatants were from the UK and all six – men and women alike – were in tears at the unfolding disaster. It so happens that my paternal great-grandparents had fled to London from Paris in 1870 when the Prussians invaded: tri-lingual in French, German and English, they carefully gave their children names that work in all three languages: my grandfather was Emil and his siblings, two of whom I remember, were called Eugenie, Jules and Adele. Fleeing to London was a lucky move: they were Jewish and thus avoided the Holocaust. I felt proud to belong to a country that once had so generous a tradition of welcoming refugees, and am ashamed and angry at how we are now rubbishing this inheritance. I grew up with cousins in Greece, France, Italy, Switzerland and Holland and have always considered myself as much European as English.

In 2001 I published the authorised biography of Dame Iris Murdoch, the centenary of whose birth falls this year. She lived in Oxford and London but considered herself Irish; she also loved learning new languages. During the war she attempted Russian and Turkish, and around 1946–7 translated Raymond Queneau's novel *Pierrot mon ami* into English. For her own novel *The Red and the Green* in 1965, she learned some Irish. Her journals abound in quotations from Russian, German and French as well as Latin and Greek. In 1968 she gave a lecture in Italian, in October 1981 participated in a conference in French on the modern novel at the Centre Pompidou and the following year gave a short morale-boosting BBC World Service broadcast in Russian, a native speaker translating and marking stresses for her. She also planned to take Russian 'O' Level. When the Maastricht Treaty was mooted around 1992, she wrote to her MP requesting that he send her a copy. She read the Treaty, finding it long, confused and obscurely written. I hope and believe she would today have been disgusted and incredulous at the bombast, fantasy and mendacity with which the Leave campaign has been conducted and sick at heart at our pointlessly diminished future.

Europe is to be divided once again. Now it is us who will be on the painful side of the partition.

BARBARIANS

Robert Irwin

Just as Gabriel Betteredge, the eccentric servant in *The Moonstone* by Wilkie Collins, resorts to *Robinson Crusoe* to find advice on the small and great matters in life, as well as foreshadowings of the future, so I too engage in bibliomancy and habitually consult Edward Gibbons' *History of the Decline and Fall of the Roman Empire*. This is what I find:

> It is the duty of a patriot to prefer and promote the exclusive interest and glory of his native country; but a philosopher may be permitted to enlarge his views, and to consider Europe as one great republic, whose various inhabitants have attained almost the same level of politeness and cultivation. The balance of power will continue to fluctuate, and the prosperity of our own, or the neighbouring kingdoms, may be alternately exalted or depressed; but these partial events cannot essentially injure our general state of happiness, the system of arts, and laws, and manners, which so distinguish the Europeans and their colonies. [Vol. 6, Ch. 38]

Gibbon went on to ask himself whether it was possible that the Europe of his day, hardly the United Republic of Europe, but perhaps something a little like it, might not suffer the same sort of fate as the Roman Empire and fall victim to a series of barbarian invasions, before he went on to answer himself and to 'explain the probable causes of our security'. First, the 'Romans were ignorant of the extent of their danger, and the number of their enemies', whereas eighteenth-century Europe was so much better informed about the dangers that lay beyond its frontiers. Secondly, though the provinces that had been absorbed into the Roman Empire thereby enjoyed many benefits, 'this union was purchased at the loss of freedom and military spirit.' This was not the case in the Europe that Gibbon knew.

Gibbon knew Europe very well. Oxford had not suited him and he spent only a little over a year there as a student before moving to the tolerant city of Lausanne, where his mind was formed over the next five years. Subsequently he undertook the Grand Tour and in Rome in 1764 he first conceived the idea of writing *The Decline and Fall*. That book is a masterpiece of English literature, but one whose style and substance owes an enormous amount to the influence of Montesquieu, Pascal and Voltaire.

Happy Europe then! Its arts, laws and manners should continue to survive and prosper as prophesied in Gibbon's divinatory text. But the British situation is less promising and, as we drift away from Europe, I fear that we are about to enter a 'Scoundrel Time', nastier and with far graver consequences than the political situation in the America of the late fifties and early sixties that was so vividly evoked by Lillian Hellman in her book of that title. A loss of civility is already evident in the rhetoric of ruthless and ambitious politicians. I believe that the barbarians are already within our walls.

THE LESSONS OF BERLIN

Frank McDonough

I'm fascinated by Berlin. The tendencies of both the Nazi and the Cold War eras to leave ruin in their wake has fractured its geography and its ideology, leaving a city with no real centre; a collection of suburbs each with a different feel.

The area around the Brandenburg Gate provides a link to the city's Prussian history, in particular the beautifully restored Reichstag building, now the centre of the new democracy. The nearby Tiergarten is the site of a Soviet war memorial, erected in 1945, within a few months of the capture of the city. Two tanks flank a giant statue of a Soviet soldier. This is just one of many sites commemorating the city's liberation by the Allies. They are testaments all to what can be achieved through international cooperation, but also poignant reminders of what can happen when nations turn inwards and pursue selfish aims.

The Memorial to the Murdered Jews of Europe can be found close by. Designed by the New York architect Peter Eisenman, it is formed of hundreds of concrete slabs of different heights. They create an uneasy, confusing atmosphere. Here it is hard not to reflect on the dangers of scapegoating and discrimination, on how these led to genocide within living memory.

European cooperation has brought peace and prosperity to the people of Europe – to us. For me Europe is so much more than an economic trading bloc; it's an attempt to create a community that allows the free movement of not just goods but also people, ideas, music and poetry. It's a desire to collaborate so that we can protect human and employment rights as well as the environment – not just for our children but for future generations.

One day, I hope that we will return to the European Community. For now all I can feel is sorrow about leaving.

THERE BE DRAGONS

Don Boyd

On 23 June 2016, my friend, the historian Frank McDonough, and I were guests at a literary festival in Piacenza, northern Italy. In the early morning hours we were texting each other from our bedrooms, our eyes glued to betting websites showing the fluctuating online odds in the UK referendum vote.

British bookmakers have always predicted the outcome of political contests more accurately than the opinion polls. We were horrified as the odds against a remain result changed spectacularly hour by hour.

When the final numbers made it clear that our country had voted to leave the European Union, we could hardly hide our shame as we slid bleary-eyed into breakfast, apologising to all our delightful European hosts who were embarrassed on our behalf.

John Ruskin, the great Victorian art historian, said that until he had seen the Tintorettos in the Scuola San Rocco in Venice, he had known nothing about art. I revisited the *Crucifixion* there this year with my granddaughters. Like Ruskin, they were also inspired by the Carpaccios in the tiny Scuola di San Giorgio Degli Schiavoni where one panel shows England's patron Saint George slaying a dragon. I joked: has Europe become the United Kingdom's metaphorical, cultural and economic dragon?

No dragons for Frank and me to slay that morning in Piacenza for sure. Only bowls of fresh pasta and slugs of inspirational Italian grappa. 'Rock on' Visconti, Fellini, De Sica, Pasolini, Antonioni, Rossellini, and, yes, the inspiration of *La Serenissima*. I am Europe too – *per favore*!

FROM WAR TO UNDERSTANDING

Richard J. Evans

I've spent my adult life thinking and writing about Europe – mainly Germany, but also the rest of Europe, including Britain, of course. I grew up in the post-war years, when the war and its legacies were very much present in our daily lives. We lived on the fringes of London's East End, and going about Leyton, Hackney, Stratford or Walthamstow, we could see for ourselves the damage done by German bombing raids. Although the debris had long been cleared away, there were still rows of terraced houses with gaps in them, gaps in which you could see, with a rather shocking kind of intimacy, the wallpaper on upstairs bedroom walls, or the tiles in downstairs bathrooms. In my great-uncle's back garden in Ilford I played with old gas masks in the Anderson shelter that was half-buried in the soil. My parents and their friends and relations often reminisced about their experiences during the war: my mother in the Blitz, where the flames in the London dockyards turned night into day, my father in North Africa and Italy, where he remembered giving water to a thirsty Italian soldier shuffling slowly forwards in a seemingly endless line of prisoners of war.

It was the Germans who fascinated me most, of course: why had they done this to London, what had made them support Hitler, how had they eventually been defeated? These questions have stayed with me for the rest of my life. But neither I nor my parents equated Germany with Europe; after all, my father's best friend in the RAF was Jim Kaminski, a Pole who had fled the German occupation of his country to join the fight against the Nazis, and the British enthusiastically celebrated the heroic deeds of the French Resistance and the brave Norwegians who fought against Quisling and his minions.

When I went to university, graduated in History and then embarked on a doctorate on modern German history, I began to realise there were many other aspiring historians of my age who had similar thoughts and experiences. Understanding what made other European cultures tick was important to us, whether we were interested in France, Italy, Germany, Russia, Spain or any one of a number of European countries. We learned the relevant languages, read the literature, listened to the music, and, above all, lived among the people as we devoted ourselves to researching in the archives and libraries of the country whose history we were trying to understand.

An astonishing number of British historians over the past half-century and more have devoted their lives to Europe, many publishing substantial and important works in the process. It's a mistake to think that British history has been the exclusive or even the main focus of our generation of historians. And what's been so striking has been the openness to us of colleagues in the countries we've been studying, and the welcome we've received from all kinds of people there. It helped, of course, that we spoke the relevant languages. Without that ability, it would have been impossible to read the original documents we needed, or keep up with the historical literature. Many of our books have been translated into German, Italian, Russian or some other European language, and most of them have been warmly received; a few have even had a discernible influence on the way the people of those countries understand their own history.

So it's a tragedy that the UK is now heading towards isolation, with fewer and fewer young people learning foreign languages, and Britain increasingly regarded as entirely separate from the Continent – indeed, the term 'the Continent' is hardly used any more: people speak instead of 'Europe', as if Britain wasn't part of it. British history is studied and written about as if it didn't belong to a larger, European history at all. Some day this trend may be reversed and we may recover the cultural and intellectual richness that comes with the consciousness that we are all Europeans.

ON THE PLAYING FIELDS OF FIESOLE

James Hanning

Not many provincial shopkeepers get to have a political mindset named after them. As a politics student I learned about one called Pierre Poujade, who later became a politician. He had no truck with tax inspectors and little, even, to do with the central state, although he gave rise to a national movement of small business owners, called Poujadism. However, about the time the European Community was getting to its feet, Poujadisme was swept away.

Occasionally, if I am looking for a synonym for political small-mindedness, I think of Poujade. It sounds pseudy; people have not heard of him, but at the time I came across him, the word Poujadist had a particular potency. It was the early eighties and I was doing research in Italy. The building I was working in, the beautiful medieval Badia Fiesolana monastery, built on the hills overlooking Florence, had been donated by the Italian government as its part in the idealistic setting up of a research institute that might help foster cross-national studies. All the EU's member countries (and more besides) chipped in, offering bursaries to postgraduate students of law, economics, history, and social and political sciences. Because it was independent but in part Brussels-funded, it could invite the best academics, who, of course, were falling over themselves to spend a few years among the olive groves. I got in probably because there wasn't much competition for places among the standoffish Brits.

I couldn't believe my luck; it was an absurdly idyllic existence. My German supervisor called us researchers 'ze pampered kids of Europe'. Born in 1921 and later a PoW, he was well placed to judge. And how did 'ze pampered kids' respond? We laughed at, and eventually with, him, we ate and drank too much, copped off with one another, learned how to pronounce 'bruschetta' properly, told jokes celebrating the fabled dimness of Italy's *carabinieri*, wound each other up, corrected one another's faltering language skills, learned a certain amount about where British exceptionalism may and will not be excused, and generally grew up a bit.

I remember the first game of football we played together, on a grassless municipal pitch in Fiesole against a local team. We all wanted to get on, I think, but in the changing room beforehand, it wasn't clear that we would. The common language, for better or worse, was English, which aggravated a sense among the Brits of being in charge. The Italians were immaculately turned out (yes, really) and keen on deciding who would take free kicks — and there was no shortage of offers — but as we had never even seen one another play, it was going to have to be a bit rough and ready.

Some — I think from the smaller nations — smiled a lot and worried whether the showers would work. Others wondered where we were going for a drink afterwards, and were stunned when not everyone did. The Francophones chatted amicably among themselves and often, rather missing the point, talked about their academic research as they laced their boots. Later, I seem to remember the odd 'crisis meeting', when the southern

Europeans felt a Brit/Danish/German cabal was monopolising things. 'You're an excellent friend but not a very good footballer,' pointed out an Italian economist. Mercifully such candour was a rarity.

The squabbling became more muted and a soggy Euro-harmony emerged, sufficient at least to win a few games. One notably hard-fought victory, in the hills of Chianti, was against a local team of small-business owners from Greve.

Ask me specifically what I learned at the Institute from the pedantic Belgian accountant, or the Roman environmentalist, or the Dutch labour market specialist, or the brilliant Irish poly-math whose presence at seminars so terrified professors of all disciplines, or the son of a Gestapo commandant, or the Flemish economist or the Bavarian historian or the man who did his doctorate on the early years of the UEFA Cup or the former colleague of Alfred Weber or the man who harboured the exiled Alexander Dubcek or the gone-straight Provo – and I'm not sure I could tell you.

But something – apart from realising how lucky I was – rubbed off. Perhaps it was just a reminder that there was an Enlightenment, there was a war, there was a peace, there was a thing called human progress, there was a promise, twice in the twentieth century, of 'never again'. And that what I had enjoyed had been put there by idealists who felt, on balance, that cross-national collaboration was a good thing, and that fatuous, mean-spirited nationalism, on the whole, wasn't. Afterwards, we pampered kids went off and earned a proper living. Some caught the bug more than others. One much-missed friend helped set up a simi-larly soft-headed bit of thinking, the Erasmus exchange programme, from which over six million students in thirty-seven countries have benefitted. Maybe we learned that Brits have plenty to offer, but we have to engage.

The words of one recent Foreign Secretary resonate here, remaining just the sensible side of jingoism.

> In an age of anxiety and uncertainty it is surely obvious that the values of global Britain are needed more than ever. And though we can never be complacent, and though we can never take our position for granted, Churchill was right when he said that the empires of the future will be empires of the mind. And in expressing our values I believe that global Britain is a soft power superpower and that we can be immensely proud of what we are achieving.

I wonder if that former Foreign Secretary, Boris Johnson, is aware that Britain has decided to send no more students to the European University Institute, the largest and one of the most prestigious social science research organisations in Europe. How many other such bodies are we pulling out of? How many friendships will be lost while we are in the grip of our own brand of Poujadisme?

A THEORY OF LIGHT

Hugh Aldersey-Williams

'Holland', writes the English poet and MP Andrew Marvell, 'scarce deserves the name of land, / As but th' off-scouring of the British sand.'

And perhaps it does happen from time to time that some of the sand from the edges of our island, lifted by the tide and swirled around the North Sea, eventually finds itself adding to the dunes of the Dutch coast.

In the province of Holland, Marvell's contemporary, the poet and diplomat Constantijn Huygens examines the light with his imperfect eyes. Bright refractions dazzle him from each silica grain. He writes: 'The Lord's benevolence shines from every dune.'

His son, Christiaan, takes the sand, melts it into glass, and grinds the glass into lenses. He incorporates the lenses into powerful homemade telescopes, and sees for the first time not only the true shape of the rings of Saturn but also Saturn's first moon, Titan.

Observing the light refracted by crystals and inspired, perhaps, by the restless surface of the North Sea, he proposes a wave theory of light. It is correct, but the world is not ready for it.

But Christiaan Huygens' greatest achievement lies somewhere else. It is to begin the hard work of building the expectation that science is something best done internationally. He becomes the first foreign member of the Royal Society in London. Living and working in Paris, he does more than anybody else to shape the early work of the French Academy of Sciences (even though he is Dutch, even though Holland and France are at war for much of the time).

These early tendrils of connection were often broken during the three centuries of nationalism and war since Huygens' time. Successor organisations only began to be founded again in Europe after the Second World War. We are now breaking the connection again.

'If a clod be washed away by the sea, Europe is the less,' John Donne had written, not long before Marvell and Constantijn Huygens, the words sandwiched between more famous lines about islands and tolling bells.

The clod is the sand. The sand is the light. These pieces of the continent we share.

KEEPING THE FLAME ALIVE

Richard Shirreff

Spend time in the Museum of Occupation in Tallinn and the KGB Museum in Vilnius and you'll begin to understand what a Europe whole and free really means. In Tallinn, read the accounts of deportation of whole families to the Soviet Gulag and how few returned, or in Vilnius shiver in the chilling atmosphere of the KGB torture chambers. Still in Vilnius, visit the Parliament building where, in the winter of 1991, unarmed demonstrators barricaded themselves against the besieging Soviet army protected only by a scratch group of volunteers led and organised by Arvydas Pocius, a former wrestling coach. Arvydas Pocius became Lithuanian Chief of Defence Staff and is now his country's ambassador in Romania. And at a time when we in Western Europe were focused only on the break-up of former Yugoslavia and did nothing to help them, the people of Estonia, Latvia and Lithuania fought for their freedom from the Soviet Union and then protected it by linking hands across their Eastern frontiers. Truly, three nations who understood the price of freedom and were prepared to pay the costs to become indissolubly a part of the European community of free nations.

Europe is not about Brussels bureaucrats or the Common Fisheries or Agricultural Policy. The single market lays down essential freedoms and has been fundamental to building peace in Northern Ireland. But more than that, Europe is an idea, a vision, a reality which has submerged nationalist rivalries and rendered the blood-letting of the last millennia unthinkable.

Europe is about peace, individual liberty, democracy and the rule of law; about building bridges rather than pulling up the drawbridge. In an imperfect world it is an ideal built by men and women determined never to repeat the carnage of the first half of the twentieth century. We owe it to them to keep the flame alive.

THEM AND US

Ranulph Fiennes

In the sixties I spent four of my years of military service during the Cold War as a Troop Commander of the seventy-tonne Conqueror tanks in the Royal Scots Grey Cavalry Regiment.

My uncle had been killed at the age of twenty-one in the First World War fighting with the Gordon Highlanders against the Germans in France.

My father was killed in 1943 while commanding the Royal Scots Greys and fighting the Nazis in Italy.

My years of preparing for tank warfare against Soviet Russia and the armies of the Warsaw Pact countries involved wholesale commitment to working alongside the (West) Germans, the French and all our other West European allies. We were defending not just our Britain but our Europe, perhaps with our lives. Through the previous centuries we had fought the French and the Germans, but that was in the past. Our Europe was now that of *our* European Union and whoever threatened us was our enemy. Details of every differing trade commitment or political wrangling between the various EU states never affected my attitude towards the 'them and us' state of my thinking. And whatever the currently unpredictable outcome of the Brexit negotiations may turn up, I sincerely hope we stay good friends with our current European allies no matter how our trading arrangements may alter.

RECKLESS WITH
OTHERS' HEARTS

EUROPE

Melvyn Bragg

The British are fundamentally European. Our language is basi-cally old German (quite early on re-christened as old English). The Vikings brought us chunks of Norse, especially to the North of England. The French, after the Conquest, donated layer on layer of language. Meanwhile, from the Roman conquest through the Roman Catholic Church and the development of classical studies, Latin has seamed its way throughout our vocabulary and our sentences.

When Churchill called for a United States of Europe after the Second World War he was adjusting two thousand years of conflict. The notion of a United Europe and the actuality of uniting Europe has so far been an overwhelming success. It has virtually halted what were interminable wars on the continent of Europe in which the English, Welsh and Scots were often only too happy to participate. It has provided a federation able to stand up to the might of America and China now that its own Empire has drained away. It provides formal alliances in science, for instance, which are world class and of enormous benefit to us. Its free-roaming policy liberated and educated young and old. Because of its perceived constitutional stability and democratic traditions, Britain stood for something valuable within the European group and was prepared to support it with intelligence and force.

The right-wing coup which has occurred, a blustering contemptible mixture of empty yearnings for past 'glories', lies and ignorant expectations of the global economy, have now cut us off from what was an invaluable source of fertility. For fifty per cent of the population in Britain it is unbearable to watch this unique process of self-harm being led by those who will not suffer.

Meanwhile, now that we have decided to split away, despite advice to the contrary from an army of experts and well-wishers, we can begin to experience the full impact of the loss.

To be marooned. To be isolated between power-blocs in which we have no stake, wilfully turning our backs on the riches of France, Germany, Italy, Spain, Holland and twenty-two other countries whose complex inter-connected traditions make Europe the most civilised and culturally rich area in the world! It's a disaster and will be a case of lasting loss and sadness. And anger.

WHENEVER I HEAR THE WORD *EUROPE*

A.L. Kennedy

Whenever I hear the word *Europe* I remember a UK Foreign Secretary addressing a polyglot audience of sincere academics. He quipped that he hoped nothing as terrible as training for the London Marathon ever happened to them. We were in Prague, not long after it became the capital of the Czech Republic. My country's representative had no idea, literally no idea, of anything unpleasant that might have happened to the audience staring up at him in the skin-crawling silence.

There comes a time when you know too much about your flag, when the sight of it sickens you.

Whenever I hear the word *Europe* I think of the ranks of British lawyers working to re-establish the rule of law after Nazism tore it up into blood and body parts. Britain helped lay the foundation of the the European Convention on Human Rights, memorialising how wrong human beings can go and how to stop them. Now my country is full of bleating, tiny men in suits who can't wait to kill the unfit, who long for uniforms. They whine on behalf of my country that European Human Rights law is an alien imposition.

Whenever I hear the word *Europe* I think of the mobility of people, the unstoppable richness that makes new art, new language, new food, new anything and everything, makes new hope out of desperate flight. I think of a refuge, I consider a communal memory of the human actions necessary to bring about positive change.

Whenever I hear the word *Europe* I know it names a choice between building and destroying, makes that manifest. When Europe chooses to build, when Europe saves its people, when Europe makes all of its people part of its project, it shows that any killing field can come to sleep in peace.

Whenever I hear the word *Europe* I think of all the British people who don't vote in European elections and claim that the EU is full of the unelected. Idiocy is fashionable where I live. It echoes. Idiocy, pride, fear – they make us turn our backs on all Europe's mechanisms set in place to maintain civil stability. We are dancing towards civil war to a fantasy swing band – all the 1940s hits.

Whenever I hear the word *Europe* I remember an historically illiterate mob of charlatans claiming to represent my country. They turned their backs on the European Parliament, the Parliament that pays them, the Parliament in which they will do no work. Their actions echoed the Nazis, that other, weaker Parliament, those other, notorious Weimar backs. Of course, they crave salutes and fatal new powers, the respect that shattering stupidity can never earn. They worship a withered confusion of Empire, Churchillian poses and fascist ideology. They live abroad. They have 'foreign' names. They scramble for EU passports. They short the pound and British stocks. They live in a fever dream of contradictions and unending hate.

Whenever I hear the word *Europe* I remember the allies and allies and allies without whom Britain would never have survived either World War. I remember the freedom fighters, the Polish fighter pilots, the families hiding fugitives, radios, books, beliefs. I remember the children thrown alive into burning pits, the naked lovers embracing in gas chambers amidst the screaming. I remember the inverted morality, the murdering doctors, the ranting press, the hanging lawyers. I remember the death industries, the cruelty, mass delusion, mass suicide. And Europe remembers, too. Europe remembers how to shut hell back in its box, how to bury the box. Britain is digging, digging deeper every day, looking for new murders to commit.

Whenever I hear the word *Europe* I want to apologise.

Whenever I hear the word *Europe* I want to weep.

Whenever I hear the word *Europe* I feel at home. Homes are never perfect, but they are home. They are always home.

THE BREXIT POEM

Alan Moore

I wrote this verse the moment that I heard
the good news that we'd got our language back
Whence I, in a misjudged racial attack,
Kicked out French, German and Italian words, and then I . . .

In July 2016 slightly more than half the population after a campaign of ridiculous disinformation voted to leave the European Union.

Leaving came as a surprise to everybody, even the ones who voted for it. People didn't really expect their leave vote to do anything. It was a wildly misguided protest.

As my mate Stewart Lee said, making a protest vote in the elections is the same as turning up to a Holiday Inn, deciding you don't like your room, and shitting the bed as a protest and then realising that you're going to sleep all night in a shitted bed.

The world inexorably gets more and more complex, as information technology accelerates. People who can see the boundaries disappearing and feel frightened and exposed, are going to desperately try to turn the clock back to a simpler time, some 'golden age' in the fifties. Nostalgia and sentiment are two of the things that lead most directly to the fascist and populist movements that we are seeing around the world today.

With so much chaos, someone will do something stupid. And when they do, things will turn very nasty. We are very much approaching a massive turning point in the culture. It reminds me of a hundred years ago at the time of the First World War, when the modern world was just starting to happen.

Let us work together towards a future that ordinary people could actually live in. It is time for this horrific and inhuman nonsense to stop.

ONCE UPON A TIME, HOSPITALS BECAME HAVENS

Irenosen Okojie

I have spent a lot of time in hospitals. My younger sister has epilepsy, a condition which has rocked our worlds in many ways. Over the years, I have sat in day rooms anxiously awaiting her various scan and test results, nervously riffling through magazines, pacing up and down the corridors trying not to let myself cave in to a terrible feeling of helplessness. I have hovered by vending machines making a mental note of the latest research I had unearthed or in the consultancy room with her during her many appointments, wondering how I would translate into some form of light, some positive that the doctors have said yet again there is no cure, that her seizures may or may not get better, that her quality of life would depend on a cocktail of medications with side effects difficult to curtail.

At every one, I would think about how each session felt like a kind of reckoning to overcome. Hospitals have a mysterious power: a place to nurse, contain; a space of change and transition, a twilight-zone refuge where miracles can happen. My complicated relationship with them is threefold; oscillating between sadness, relief and certain inevitability.

But they have saved us. Without that structure in place, I have no idea how I would have managed my sister's condition. Every now and again, I think of the ambulance men who picked her up then took her to the hospital after she had a seizure on the street, staying with her until she came to; the nurse who told us jokes as a distraction when she was being weaned off one medication overnight, her body jerking repeatedly while I held her hand; the doctor who spent time reassuring us when she wept after a very tough follow-up meeting.

I am grateful for hospitals, good doctors, nurses and ambulance staff who care about what they do. In Britain's hospitals, I discovered the power of the human spirit to prevail, the kindness and empathy of unsung heroes. I am grateful for a National Health Service that, although flawed, provides free healthcare for everyone. This is an amazing thing about the UK. I hope we do not negotiate it away in some short-sighted Brexit deal. It is a matter of life and death for some.

FIFTY YEARS

Daragh Carville

I was born in 1969, the year the Troubles began.

In August that year, on the Cathedral Road, Armagh, the street I grew up on, a young man called John Gallagher was heading home after a night out at the Shambles Corner, a part of town known then, as now, for its pubs. How often have I staggered out that road myself, three sheets to the wind? Only, that night, John Gallagher stumbled into a riot. There had been a Civil Rights march in the city earlier that day and now the crowd of protesters – all unarmed civilians – was squaring up against a platoon of the auxiliary police force known as the B Specials. The police opened fire and John Gallagher was killed, shot in the back. He left behind him a widow and three young children under the age of seven.

There's some dispute about who the first victim of the Troubles was, but in Armagh that dubious honour is accorded to John Gallagher. On the day he died, 14 August 1969, riots were also raging in Belfast and Derry, the first British troops were deployed, and Northern Ireland entered the long darkness of a conflict that, over the next thirty years, would claim more than three thousand lives and devastate countless more.

We lived in Armagh but as my dad is from Monaghan, we crossed the border regularly, moving between jurisdictions, stopping at checkpoints, flagged down by heavily armed squaddies with strange English accents. As kids, me and my brothers would sit clenched in silence in the back seat as Dad handed over his driving licence and answered their questions about who we were and where we were going and why.

I left Northern Ireland at eighteen, moving first to England, then to France, luxuriating (or so it seems to me now) in the opportunities afforded first by student grants – though, even then, grants were being whittled down and fees were on the horizon – and then by the principle of Freedom of Movement within the EU. I moved back to Northern Ireland in the mid-nineties, as the peace process took hold, with 'talks about talks' gradually giving way to actual talk. And then finally, after a long and tortuous process – peace broke out. And that's how it felt, paradoxically: a sudden outpouring of peace, a joyous eruption of – ordinary life. Of decency. Of normality. How long ago that all seems now. How distant.

I keep thinking about those questions the soldiers used to ask at checkpoints and border crossings. Who are you? Where are you from? Where are you going? Questions of identity and belonging. Questions we thought – perhaps naively – we had put behind us.

The Good Friday Agreement enshrined the right of every citizen in Northern Ireland to define their own identity, as British, or Irish, or both. In all the talk of Brexit and the backstop and alternative arrangements and technological solutions, this is what is being missed, at least by Boris Johnson and his fellow fanatics. The border question is not ultimately about trade, it's not about money. It's not about goods and lorries and standards and specifications. It's about who you are, and where you're from, and where you're going. It's about identity. And there are no technological solutions to questions of identity.

THE LOVE YOU TAKE

FROM GO-KARTS TO MBAS

Will Hutton

I fell in love with Europe in August 1962 – in a pedal go-kart on Blakenberge's sweeping esplanade on the Belgian coast. I couldn't believe the careless freedom given to twelve-year-old boys to roam anywhere along the front. And then afterwards back to the tiny hotel where a friendly Madame together with a huge pre-war apron served up fantastic *frites*. With everything! My brother and I were in heaven. They certainly did things differently in Europe. And it was so much more fun!

When we came home, I unearthed the holiday brochures and spent happy hours pondering where next in Europe we could go. I even forgave my father his embarrassing habit of buying German men his own age a drink saying that Europeans should never fight again and how much he respected German soldiers. Meanwhile there was I having to play with their children, unable to speak a word. When given the fateful choice that September to learn GCE Latin or German, I opted for German – which would later stand in my way of going to Cambridge to study History, as Latin was then a prerequisite. But I remember looking out of the classroom window at the tall trees at the bottom of the play-ground thinking it was a signal of being part of the future. Britain was already talking about joining the 'Common Market' and I'd been to Europe. There really wasn't a choice. Although

History at Cambridge never happened, I have never regretted my schoolboy choice.

It's a love affair that has lasted all my life. At twenty-seven I needed to break out of a stifling career in stockbroking: it paid ridiculously well but a lifetime of buying and selling pre-existing financial assets was futile and ultimately purposeless. An MBA at INSEAD – l'Institut European des Affaires – was my way out, this time my admission helped by my proud German GCE rather than blocked. A new building at the edge of the forest of Fontainebleau, where the coffee and chocolate croissants were beyond belief, became my intellectual home for a year.

There Ineke Louwers, the wife of my new Belgian friend Bookie, took me aside one day and told me how much she admired my English writing. 'You're the best writer in the group,' she said. 'Write up your group's discussions.' To my astonishment the group concurred and I became their rapporteur. It convinced me that, rather than business, finance or consultancy, my real métier was going to be economic journalism. To this day I remain virtually the only INSEAD *ancien* to have made a career in journalism.

INSEAD also taught me about the need for patient, long-term capital in business, and the importance of real-life public financial institutions – such as the KfW (the state-owned development bank) in Germany or the Caisse des Depots in France – that all over Europe ensured their economies had that crucial lifeblood. Suddenly I understood what lay behind Keynes's magisterial and insightful critique of capitalism (like me, he was dismissive of the role of the British financial markets), not least because he had first-hand experience of their fecklessness, having speculated in them. My mission was clear: to be an economic journalist who would try to explain this to the British. My first book, *The State We're In*, was born.

The friends I made at INSEAD have been lifelong. We may have come from all over Europe, but we were and are peas in a pod. We are fellow Europeans with the same dreams and heart-aches. My father buying drinks for ex-German soldiers no longer seems embarrassing but something I remember and cherish him most for.

Later I became a rapporteur for the EU's Kok Commission – a wonderful, wise ex-Dutch Prime Minister – into how the EU could develop a twenty-first-century economy. In effect it was a recipe for Britain – building a Europe-wide economy and society that would try to meld the best of British-style flexibility, inventiveness and entrepreneurialism with European long termism, social solidarity and sense of the commonweal. It is my manifesto for Britain. Are my life experience and beliefs so unusual as to be dismissed by Brexiters as unpatriotic quirks? I think not. Instead I believe that they are quintessentially British, that mine is a story that any one of us could have had, given the same chances. To love Europe is to love Britain. To love Britain is to love Europe.

THE ORIGINAL MEANING OF 'CATHOLIC'

Peter Stanford

There are plenty of reasons why so many British people today think of themselves as Europeans: by birth, by background, and by educational, social, economic or cultural inclination. For the one-in-twelve of us Brits who are (or have been brought up as) Catholics, there is another. All those years of Mass attendance and RE lessons have at their best left us hardwired to look beyond national boundaries and consider ourselves part of something universal – the original meaning of the word 'catholic', as first used by Christians at the start of the second century CE.

Once, that bigger connection was given practical expression by the unifying (if largely incomprehensible) use of Latin in every Catholic church across the globe. The language was changed to the vernacular in the sixties, but that core sense of being part of a group of people that transcended borders didn't go away; it simply had to find another expression. For many British Catholics, that came from joining, in 1973, the wider European community: sharing goals, ambitions and beliefs, moving among each other freely and recognising a common heritage.

By the time I was growing up Catholic in Liverpool in the 1970s, the ghosts of the English and Scottish Reformations, which had made Catholics a hated minority, had finally been exorcised, but there was still a trace of the old, ugly sectarianism between Protestants and Catholics that had once scarred the city. Can I really remember in my teenage years seeing the Orange marchers at the Pier Head one 12 July, spitting poison about the Pope being the anti-Christ? It seems impossible now, but I know I did.

More broadly, though, in the decades since, we left-footers (once a term of abuse, now a phrase we have detoxified) have successfully been reintegrated. We are now accepted as simultaneously British *and* members of a global congregation. What more quintessentially reassuring and English figure was there than Cardinal Basil Hume, a high-profile, widely admired (beyond the pews) leader of the Catholic Church in England and Wales until his death in 1999? How little did it matter that his mother was French, his father Scottish, and his boss based in Rome?

In my own case that seamless connection between what I believed and what I was, became a love affair with Europe. I spent my student summers living in Rome, where going into churches to light candles made me, for the first time, part of a majority culture that existed not only there, but across a whole continent.

Those experiences must have had some bearing on how, in my twenties, I found myself a journalist and an editor at British Catholic newspapers. I spent my time and column inches enthusiastically reporting what was going on in the progressive European church, in the forlorn hope that it would encourage our domestic, still timid, native variety of Catholicism to start seeing itself as properly European in the best sense of the word.

Fast forward to today, and such uninterrupted, instinctive exchange, that outward-looking, effortless, beyond-boundaries pursuit of shared religious and spiritual beliefs that for decades has chimed with a political and economic vision of a shared, just and equal European future, is suddenly at risk. Alongside all the other potential losses that could follow Brexit, and which I publicly lament alongside millions of others, this is the one that I am also privately mourning – and at the same time praying for a miracle.

ENOUGH

Kapka Kassabova

Though I didn't know it, and despite the Iron Curtain, I grew up in Bulgaria as a deeply, old-fashionedly pan-European. As a child, I knew how to scale resiny fir trees in the mountains, how to gather wild berries in late summer and preserve them, taught by my grandmothers, and how to pick lime-blossom and elder-flower in spring and make tea and cordial for hayfever, how to make yogurt – and that family mealtimes were sacred. On television, I watched Russian war films, soulful Italian and French dramas, zany Czechoslovak series, and even the odd Hollywood blockbuster about the Roman Empire, like *Spartacus* (who, having been born in today's Bulgaria, was clearly European).

Emigrating as a teenager to New Zealand, and later as an adult to Scotland, I was surprised to find that this had not been the formative experience of my generation in the Anglo-American-Antipodean world. That they had a whole other world of songs, jokes, and TV characters to quote, and that 'panto-mime' in Britain meant something very different from the art of Marcel Marceau.

No matter what happens to Europe, I have seen the essential Europe I love and carry in my bones, a continent whose secret histories and inflections weave themselves into everything I write and everything I am.

Europe of forested seasons and ancient languages spoken by people with faces tattooed with harshness and forgiveness.

Europe where borders and peoples have moved across the land like spilled mercury, leaving memory stains.

Euro-Africa of the seedy ports where the red wind of the Sahara blows in.

Europe that rises from the ashes of its own murderous madness.

Europe of neighbours and intermarriages, not militarised borders.

Balkan, Eurasian, oldest of Europe, where the confluence of East and West is a tangle of rivers running into the Aegean.

Europe not of the engorged imperial capitals, but of the pot-holed roads between villages with names difficult to pronounce, of fishing towns and islands with lanolin jumpers, of lonely coastal cottages, of Orcadian graffiti scratched by Vikings in a moment of drunken immortality.

I struggle to separate the Europeanness of the British Isles from the rest of European Westerndom. To me, a child of the European East, they are civilisationally one. And if we go back far enough, everything came to Europe from the East: people, ideas, wine, wheat, gold, prophets.

Travelling along the lethal Iron Curtain of my childhood, now on history's scrap-heap, I saw this: the destiny of all walls is to crumble, no matter how many lives they smite and how permanent they look. A border crumbles and you see that the neighbour looks like you. Borders are mirrors in which we see our true reflection.

This is my difficult Europe – a continent of lessons so hard-won they bankrupt us, of vanishing borders, of last-ditch chances and unbelievable stories of escape, of people like you and me and our grandparents, who carry the heartbreak of four wars on European soil within just three generations: the Second World War, the Greek Civil War (1946–49), the Yugoslav Wars (1991– 2001) and the Cold War (1945–89). This is my Europe – where so much suffering has been carried by so many for so long, that being human must surely be enough, for us to continue. It is enough for me. Enough.

ABROAD-THOUGHTS, FROM HOME.

OH, TO BE IN EUROPE,
NOW THAT BREXIT'S HERE,
FILLING MY THOUGHTS WITH MEMORIES OF HAPPIER TIMES;

THAT FIRE-FLY STROLL THROUGH SIENNESE VINEYARDS
BELOW THE CASTLE OF THE FOUR TOWERS,

DRIVING DOWN LONG STRAIGHT CYPRESS TREE LINED ROADS
PAST WITCH-HAT TURRETED CHATEAUX
IN THAT OLD VW BEETLE, MORE RUST THAN CAR,
THEN WAKING UP IN THE DORDOGNE AND DRINKING
COFFEE FROM A BOWL, LOOKING ACROSS THAT
OAK TREE FORESTED VALLEY,

BEING DRUNK ON AQUA VITE AND PARLIAMENTARY
HOSPITALITY IN CHRISTMAS CARD COPENHAGEN,
WALKING THROUGH THE COBBLED STREETS OF PRAGUE
AND CHANCING UPON THOSE MUCHA TERMINAL GODDESSES,
FADED AND FORGOTTEN ON THE FAÇADE OF THE RAILWAY STATION,

SITTING ON THAT PALAZZO BALCONY WATCHING
THE BOATS GO BY ON THE GRAND CANAL,
FEELING LIKE A GUGGENHEIM,

BUT MOST OF ALL, FEELING,
WITH THE REMEMBERED EXHILARATION OF AN INTER-RAILING
STUDENT, CHILD OF THE SEVENTIES, THREE DAY WEEK AND
WINTER OF DISCONTENT,
EUROPEAN...

NOT SMALL, ROTUND, WAISTCOAT CORSETTED, ROAST BEEF
BREATHED, FOAM-FLECK LIPPED, RED FACED, CLIFF TOP
FIST-SHAKING, JOHN BULLISH, LITTLE ENGLANDER,

BUT EUROPEAN.

ONE DAY MY CHILDREN WILL KNOW THAT
FEELING AGAIN.

CHRIS RIDDELL.

A LOVE LETTER TO EUROPE

Neil Gaiman

Dear Europe,

I loved feeling part of you. That feeling that we were together, our differences combining to make something bigger than either of us. Something unique, something neither of us could have been on our own. We were workmates who became closer than that.

I loved knowing that, even though we were a couple, we were still very much ourselves. You weren't asking me to change the things about myself that I didn't want to.

I loved you when they lied about you. I loved the things you gave me: the peace and the prosperity, the knowledge that in a fight you'd have my back. I loved that you saw me as odd, ill-fitting, awkward in our relationship, but you accepted what made me special, even seemed to appreciate it.

With you, I could go anywhere. I loved the people you brought into my world, and loved going places with you. I heard things, tasted things, delighted in things I would never have encountered without you. If we had children, they had so many places they would have been at home, so many places they could have lived.

I don't know why I'm leaving you, but I know how it goes. I said things I can't take back. I did things I regret. I wish things could be like they were.

That's all I want for both of us.

That things could be like they used to be.

But you'll be fine without me, my love. How I'll be, without you, I'm not so sure . . .

still love

Neil

CONTRIBUTORS

HUGH ALDERSEY-WILLIAMS studied natural sciences at Cambridge. He is the author of several books exploring science, design and architecture, including *Periodic Tales, Tides* and *The Adventures of Sir Thomas Browne in the 21st Century*. His next book, *Dutch Light: Christiaan Huygens and the Making of Science in Europe*, will be published in 2020.

PHILIP ARDAGH is the Roald Dahl Funny Prize-winning author of over 100 children's titles. A series of letters he wrote to his nephew, Ben, became the book *Awful End*, translated into over thirty-five languages. He collaborated with Sir Paul McCartney on his first children's book.

JAKE ARNOTT is the author of seven novels. His first, *The Long Firm*, was adapted as an award-winning drama series for BBC2. His latest, *The Fatal Tree*, is set in the underworld of eighteenth-century London.

PATRICIA ATKINSON has lived in south-western France for thirty years, having left her city job to work in the vineyards. She is the author of the bestselling *The Ripening Sun*, which describes her transition from novice amateur to expert, award-winning winemaker, and of *La Belle Saison*, a meditation on the simple luxuries of good food, wine and friendship.

PAUL ATTERBURY is primarily a writer whose books have been about art, antiques and design, travel, railways and canals, Victorian culture, France and the First World War. He has also been for many years one of the expert team on BBC TV's *Antiques Roadshow*.

NICK BARRATT is an author, broadcaster and historian best known for his work on the BBC's *Who Do You Think You Are?* He is an honorary associate professor of public history at the University of Nottingham, an Associate Director, Collections and Engagement, at the University of London's Senate House Library and a teaching fellow at the University of Dundee. His book *The Forgotten Spy* tells the story of his great uncle – Stalin's first mole in Whitehall – and he has previously written on subjects as diverse as the story of Greater London and the Titanic.

MARY BEARD is a professor of classics at Newnham College, Cambridge, and the classics editor of the *TLS*. She has earned world-wide academic acclaim. Her previous books include the bestselling, Wolfson Prize-winning *Pompeii*, *The Parthenon*, *Confronting the Classics* and *SPQR*. Her blog has been collected in the books *It's a Don's Life* and *All in a Don's Day*.

RICHARD BEARD is the author of *Acts of the Assassins*, which was shortlisted for the Goldsmiths prize, *The Day That Went Missing*, winner of the Penn Ackerley prize and the widely acclaimed *Becoming Drusilla*. He was formerly director of the

National Academy of Writing in London, and is now a visiting professor at the University of Tokyo and has a Creative Writing Fellowship at the University of East Anglia. He is an optimistic opening batsman for the Authors' Cricket Club.

ZOË BEATY has been a journalist for ten years, specialising in news, politics, feminism, mental health and current affairs in her most recent post as news editor of *The Pool*.

JEFFREY BOAKYE is a writer and teacher originally from Brixton, London, with a particular interest in issues surrounding education, race and popular culture. His books include *Black, Listed: Black British Culture Explored* and *Hold Tight: Black Masculinity, Millennials, and the Meaning of Grime*.

DON BOYD is a Scottish film director, producer and screenwriter, whose films include the multi-directorial opera film *Aria*; *My Kingdom*, a contemporary *King Lear* adaptation starring Richard Harris and Lynn Redgrave; Derek Jarman's *War Requiem* with Lawrence Olivier and Tilda Swinton; and the BBC Storyville BIFA-nominated *Andrew and Jeremy Get Married*. He is also the author of *Margot's Secrets*.

MELVYN BRAGG is a writer and broadcaster who has for many years hosted the discussion programme *In Our Time* on BBC Radio 4. His novels include *The Hired Man*, for which he won the *Time/Life* Silver Pen Award; *Without A City Wall*, winner of the John Llewellyn Rhys Prize; *The Soldier's Return*, winner of the WHSmith Literary Award; *A Son of War* and *Crossing the Lines*, both of which were longlisted for the Man Booker Prize;

A Place in England, which was longlisted for the Lost Man Booker Prize; and most recently *Love Without End*.

GYLES BRANDRETH is a writer, broadcaster, former MP and government whip. Currently a reporter on BBC TV's *The One Show* and a regular on Radio 4's *Just a Minute*, his bestselling books include *Word Play*, *The 7 Secrets of Happiness*, *Have You Eaten Grandma?* and acclaimed Victorian detective stories *The Oscar Wilde Murder Mysteries*.

KATHLEEN BURK is Professor Emerita of Modern and Contemporary History at University College London as well as a commentator and radio panellist. She is the author of several distinguished scholarly books on the US and its interventions in the rest of the world, including *Old World, New World* and *The Lion and the Eagle*. She also writes on wine.

JAMIE BUXTON is a translator and writer. He has published eight novels, four on gothic and horror themes, four for young people. He is currently working on a Druids vs Romans fantasy adventure and a World War Two thriller involving artists, fascists and the English countryside. He lived in Berlin from the spring of 1964 to the winter of 1966.

SIMON CALLOW made his stage debut in 1973 and came to prominence in a critically acclaimed performance as Mozart in the original stage production of Peter Shaffer's *Amadeus*. He is well known for a series of one-man shows that have toured internationally and featured subjects such as Charles Dickens, Oscar Wilde, William Shakespeare, Jesus and Richard Wagner. Among his many film roles is the much-loved character Gareth in *Four Weddings and a Funeral*. He is the author of acclaimed biographies of Orson Welles, Charles Laughton and Charles Dickens, as well as bestselling memoirs *Love is Where it Falls*, *My Life in Pieces* and *Being an Actor*.

PHILIP CARR-GOMM is a psychologist and leader of the Order of Bards, Ovates & Druids. He is the author of over a dozen books, including *Sacred Places, A Brief History of Nakedness*, and the novel *The Prophecies*.

DARAGH CARVILLE is a playwright and screenwriter from Armagh, Northern Ireland. The first series of his crime drama *The Bay* was broadcast on ITV in 2019. Other TV credits include *Being Human* and *The Smoke*. His films are *Middletown* and *Cherrybomb*. Plays include *Language Roulette*, *This Other City* and *The Life and Times of Mitchell and Kenyon*. Daragh Carville has won the Meyer Whitworth and Stewart Parker awards. He teaches Creative Writing at Birkbeck, University of London.

BRIAN CATLING was born in London in 1948. He is a former Professor of Fine Art at the Ruskin School, Oxford, and is an acclaimed performance artist and sculptor. His work often takes the form of video or live performance – events which often defy categorisation. A Royal Academician, he is exhibiting paintings and etchings at this year's Summer Exhibition. His acclaimed *Vorrh* trilogy is followed this year by *Earwig*, which is being filmed by Lucile Hadžihalilović.

SHAMI CHAKRABARTI is Britain's leading human rights campaigner. Shadow Attorney General and a member of the House of Lords, Chakrabarti is an Honorary Professor of Law at the University of Bristol and the University of Manchester, an Honorary Fellow at Lucy Cavendish College, Cambridge and Mansfield College, Oxford, and a Master of the Bench of Middle Temple. Chakrabarti was the Director of Liberty, the National Council for Civil Liberties from 2003 to 2016, and the Chancellor of the University of Essex from 2014 to 2017. She is the author of *On Liberty,* an impassioned defence of human rights, published in 2014, and *Of Women,* a feminist argument for affirmative action in 2017.

DR TOM CHATFIELD is a British writer, broadcaster and tech philosopher. His books exploring digital culture are published in over two dozen languages. His latest non-fiction book, *Critical Thinking,* is a bestselling textbook in its field; and his debut novel, *This is Gomorrah,* was a *Sunday Times* thriller of the month.

CHRIS CLEAVE is a *New York Times* #1 bestselling novelist whose books are published in forty countries. His work explores the ways in which people recover from heartbreak, madness and trauma. He is currently training as a psychotherapist. His most recent novel, *Everyone Brave is Forgiven,* is set in European theatres of the Second World War.

MARK COCKER is one of Britain's most respected writers on nature and contributes regularly to the *Guardian,* the *New Statesman* and the *Spectator.* His twelve books, including *Our Place* and *Birds and People,* have been shortlisted for numerous awards. *Crow Country* was shortlisted for the Samuel Johnson prize and won the New Angle Prize. In 2016 he was awarded an Honorary Doctorate of Literature from the University of East Anglia, where he has recently placed his archive.

PETER J. CONRADI is the author of the widely acclaimed biography *Iris Murdoch: A Life* and has edited two collections of her writings: *Existentialists and Mystics* and *A Writer at War*. He has also written studies of the Welsh March (*At the Bright Hem of God*), of becoming a Buddhist (*Going Buddhist*) and a life of the soldier-poet Frank Thompson (*A Very English Hero*) who was murdered in Bulgaria in 1944. His most recent book is *Family Business: A Memoir*, chosen as non-fiction book of the month by *The Bookseller*.

HEATHER COOPER is the author of *Stealing Roses*, set on the Isle of Wight in the 1860s. Her past jobs include working for the National Trust and the NHS.

FRANK COTTRELL BOYCE is an award-winning author and screenwriter. *Millions*, his debut children's novel, won the CILIP Carnegie Medal. He is also the author of *Chitty Chitty Bang Bang Flies Again*, *Cosmic*, *Framed* and *The Astounding Broccoli Boy*. His books have been shortlisted for a multitude of prizes, including the *Guardian* Children's Fiction Prize, the Whitbread Children's Fiction Award (now the Costa Book Award) and the Roald Dahl Funny Prize. *Sputnik's Guide to Life on Earth* was shortlisted for the 2017 CILIP Carnegie Medal and selected for the inaugural W H Smith Tom Fletcher Book Club. He was the writer of the Opening Ceremony for the London 2012 Olympics.

ROGER CROWLEY is a best-selling narrative historian, focused on writing page-turning history based on first-hand eyewitness accounts. He is the author of a trilogy of books on the Mediterranean world and the contest between Islam and Christianity: *Constantinople: The Last Great Siege*, *Empires of the Sea* – a *Sunday Times* History Book of the Year and *New York Times* bestseller – and *City of Fortune* on Venice, as well as *Conquerors* – a history of the Portuguese discovery of the world. His most recent book, *Accursed Tower*, is about the crusades.

DAVID CRYSTAL, OBE, is a writer, editor, lecturer, broadcaster and honorary professor of linguistics at the University of Bangor. He has written over a hundred books, including *Sounds Appealing: The Passionate Story of English Pronunciation*, *We Are Not Amused: Victorian Views on Pronunciation as Told in The Pages of Punch*, *The Story of Be: A Verb's-eye View of the English Language* and *Making Sense: The Glamorous Story of English Grammar*.

ABI CURTIS is Professor of Creative Writing at York St John University. She has published poetry widely and her first novel *Water & Glass* came out in 2017. She has been the recipient of a Somerset Maugham Award.

WILLIAM DALRYMPLE is the bestselling author of the Wolfson Prize-winning *White Mughals*, *The Last Mughal*, which won the Duff Cooper Prize, the Hemingway and Kapuscinski Prize-winning *Return of a King*, and recent bestseller *The Anarchy*. A frequent broadcaster, he has written and presented three television series, one of which won the Grierson Award for Best Documentary Series at BAFTA. He writes regularly for the

New York Review of Books, the *New Yorker* and the *Guardian* and in 2018 he was presented with the prestigious President's Medal by the British Academy for outstanding literary achievement.

LINDSEY DAVIS is a multi-award-winning author whose Falco books are hugely popular all over the world. She is past Chair of the Crimewriters' Association and The Society of Authors, and a Vice-President of the Classical Association.

DAME MARGARET DRABBLE is the author of nineteen novels, including *A Summer Bird-Cage*, *The Millstone*, *The Peppered Moth*, *The Red Queen*, *The Sea Lady* and, most recently, the highly acclaimed *The Pure Gold Baby* and *The Dark Flood Rises*. She has written biographies, screenplays and was the editor of the *Oxford Companion to English Literature*. She was awarded the 2011 Golden PEN Award for a Lifetime's Distinguished Service to Literature.

MARK ELLEN is an award-winning writer and broadcaster who edited *Smash Hits*, *Q* and *Select*, and helped to launch *MOJO*. He stood in for John Peel on Radio One and then joined the *Old Grey Whistle Test*, becoming one of the TV presenters of Live Aid in 1985. For ten years, from 2002, he edited the much-missed music publication, *The Word*. His recently published memoir is called *Rock Stars Stole My Life!*

TRACEY EMIN was born in London in 1963, and studied at Maidstone College of Art and the Royal College of Art. She has exhibited extensively internationally, including solo and group exhibitions in Holland, Germany, Hong Kong, Japan, Australia and America. Emin represented Great Britain at the Venice Biennale in 2007 and was elected a Royal Academician in the same year. In 2011, she became the Professor of Drawing at the Royal Academy of Arts, London, and in 2013 Queen Elizabeth II appointed her Commander of the Most Excellent Order of the British Empire for her contributions to the visual arts.

RICHARD J. EVANS is Regius Professor Emeritus of History at Cambridge University and the author of many widely acclaimed books including his *Third Reich Trilogy*, *Cosmopolitan Islanders: British Historians and the European Past* and *The Pursuit of Power: Europe 1815–1914*. His work has been translated into over twenty languages, including Czech, Dutch, French, German, Greek, Italian, Polish, Romanian, Russian and Swedish. He is currently Provost of Gresham College, London.

SIMON EVANS is a stand-up comedian for whom 31 October is an even more meaningful date than for Brexit. You can find out why at his current show *Dressing for Dinner*.

MICHEL FABER's books include *The Crimson Petal and the White*, *The Fahrenheit Twins*, the Whitbread-shortlisted *Under the Skin*, and *Undying*, a collection of poetry. He has won a number of short story awards, and his last novel *The Book of Strange New Things* won the Saltire Book of the Year in 2015. A book for children is forthcoming.

SEBASTIAN FAULKS is the bestselling and award-winning author of *A Possible Life*, *Human Traces*, *On Green Dolphin*

Street, Engleby, Birdsong, A Week in December, Where My Heart Used to Beat and *Paris Echo*.

SIR RANULPH FIENNES was the first man to reach both poles by surface travel and the first to cross the Antarctic Continent unsupported. He has led over thirty expeditions, including the first polar circumnavigation of the Earth, and in 2003 he ran seven marathons in seven days on seven continents in aid of the British Heart Foundation. His bestselling books include *Captain Scott, Mad Dogs and Englishmen* and *Mad, Bad and Dangerous to Know*.

NEIL GAIMAN is the Newbery, Carnegie Medal, Hugo and Nebula award-winning author of *American Gods, The Graveyard Book, Neverwhere* and *The Sandman*. Most recently he showran his adaptation of Terry Pratchett and his novel *Good Omens* for Amazon and the BBC. He is Professor in the Arts at Bard College, and a United Nations Goodwill Ambassador for Refugees. He lives in the UK and the USA.

JANET GLEESON worked at Sotheby's and Bonhams auctioneers before embarking on a writing career. She is the author of three novels, *The Grenadillo Box, The Serpent in the Garden* and *The Thief-Taker*. She is also the author of the *Sunday Times* nonfiction bestsellers *The Arcanum* and *The Moneymaker*.

DAME EVELYN GLENNIE has performed worldwide with the greatest orchestras, conductors and artists, and her solo recordings are as diverse as her career on-stage. A double Grammy award winner and BAFTA nominee, Evelyn is a composer for film, television and music library companies. Evelyn was awarded an OBE in 1993 and now has nearly 100 international awards to date, including the Polar Music Prize and the Companion of Honour. Evelyn is currently embarking on the formation of the Evelyn Glennie Archive Collection. The vision is to open a centre that embodies her mission to Teach the World to Listen.

JAMES HANNING is a journalist who worked for the *Daily Mail*, the *Evening Standard* and the *Independent on Sunday*. He is the co-author, with Francis Elliott, of *David Cameron: Practically a Conservative*, and of *The News Machine*, with Glenn Mulcaire, about the phone-hacking scandal.

NICK HAYES is the author of *The Rime of the Modern Mariner*, an updating of Coleridge's famous poem, and the visual biography *Woody Guthrie and the Dust Bowl Ballads*, both of which are among the most highly regarded of recent British long-form comics. He has also published two collections of his short comics, *Lovely Grey Day* and *11 Folk Songs*. He is the founding editor of *Meat* magazine, a periodical showcasing new writing, comics, and illustration and has won two *Guardian* Media awards.

ALAN HOLLINGHURST is the author of six novels, *The Swimming-Pool Library*, *The Folding Star*, *The Spell*, *The Line of Beauty*, *The Stranger's Child* and *The Sparsholt Affair*. He has received the Somerset Maugham Award, the James Tait Black Memorial Prize for Fiction and the 2004 Man Booker Prize.

GABBY HUTCHINSON CROUCH is a comedy writer and author. Her credits include *The News Quiz*, *The Now Show*, *Dead*

Ringers and *Elephant in the Room* (Radio 4); *Horrible Histories* (CBBC) and *Newzoids* (ITV1). Her comedy fantasy novel *Darkwood* is recently published. She lives in Canterbury with her husband, two children, and a naughty cat.

WILL HUTTON is Principal of Hertford College Oxford and a columnist for the *Observer*. His bestselling books include *The State We're In*, *The World We're In*, *Them and Us* and, with Andrew Adonis, *Saving Britain*.

ROBERT IRWIN is a writer and editor whose non-fiction works include *The Arabian Nights: A Companion*, *The Alhambra* and *For Lust of Knowing: The Orientalists and Their Enemies*. His novels include *Wonders Will Never Cease* and, most recently, *My Life is Like a Fairy Tale*. He is a Fellow of the Royal Society of Literature, of the London Institute of 'Pataphysics, of the Royal Asiatic Society and of the Society of Antiquaries.

KEVIN JACKSON is an English writer, broadcaster, filmmaker and pataphysician. He was educated at the Emanuel School, Battersea, and Pembroke College, Cambridge.

HOLLY JOHNSON is an English artist, musician, and writer, best known as the lead vocalist of Frankie Goes to Hollywood. His autobiography *There's a Bone in my Flute* was published in 1994.

LIANE JONES was born in Wales and educated in England, apart from an unexpected two-and-a-half-year period when her family moved to France. In her twenties she lived in Paris and Rome, earning money as an English teacher and a supposedly bilingual secretary, while gathering the vague degree of life experience required to start writing. She has written three novels, including *The Dream Stone*, which won the Betty Trask Award, and three non-fiction books, including *A Quiet Courage*, which tells the stories of women SOE agents in France.

RUTH JONES is best known for her outstanding and award-winning television writing – BBC1's *Gavin & Stacey*, in which she played the incorrigible Nessa, and Sky 1's *Stella*, in which she played the titular role. She has won acclaim for her performances in BBC dramas *Tess of the D'Urbervilles*, *Little Dorrit* and *Hattie*, as well as comedies *Little Britain, Saxondale* and *Nighty Night*. Her debut novel *Never Greener* was a number one best-seller, and her second – *Us Three* – is out in 2020.

SAM JORDISON is the co-director of the independent publisher Galley Beggar Press, a journalist who mainly writes about books for the *Guardian*, the co-editor of the bestselling *Crap Towns* series and the author of several other works of non-fiction, including a guide to the geniuses who brought us Trump and Brexit called *Enemies of the People*.

KAPKA KASSABOVA is the author of the multi-award winning *Border: A Journey to the Edge of Europe*. Her new book is *To The Lake: A Balkan Journey of War and Peace*. She lives in the Scottish Highlands.

A.L. KENNEDY has written nine novels, six short-story collections, three books of non-fiction and three books for children and has won a variety of UK and international book awards, including a Lannan Award, the Costa Prize, the Heinrich Heine Preis, the Somerset Maugham Award and the John Llewellyn Rees Prize. She also writes for the stage, screen, TV and has created an extensive body of radio work including documentaries, monologues, dramas and essays. She also performs occasionally in one-person shows and as a stand-up comic.

PROFESSOR DAME HERMIONE LEE was President of Wolfson College from 2008 to 2017 and is Emeritus Professor of English Literature in the English Faculty at Oxford University. She is a biographer and critic whose work includes biographies of Virginia Woolf, Edith Wharton and Penelope Fitzgerald (winner of the James Tait Black Prize for Biography and one of the *New York Times* best ten books of 2014).

PRUE LEITH's long career at the heart of the British food scene has encompassed spells as a restaurateur, a chef, a cookery writer, and most recently a judge on *The Great British Bake Off*. She is the author of eight novels as well as a recent memoir, *Relish*.

PATRICK LENOX is a former diplomat who has worked in opaque, hostile and politically delicate environments in a career spanning over twenty-five years. He was posted to a number of European capitals and worked in Central and Eastern Europe, the Balkans, the Middle East and South Asia.

ROGER LEWIS, author of *Seasonal Suicide Notes*, *What Am I Still Doing Here?* and biographies of Peter Sellers, Laurence Olivier, Charles Hawtrey and Anthony Burgess, is working on two books, *Growing Up with Comedians*, and a study of Richard Burton and Elizabeth Taylor, entitled *Erotic Vagrancy*.

DAVID LINDO is 'The Urban Birder' – broadcaster, writer, speaker and tour leader. His mission is to engage city folk around the world with the environment through the medium of birds. He was recently named the seventh most influential person in wildlife by *BBC Wildlife* magazine.

DAME PENELOPE LIVELY has written many prize-winning novels for adults and children. They include: *Life in the Garden*, *Moon Tiger* (which won the 1987 Booker Prize), *The Road to Lichfield*, *According to Mark*, *Heat Wave*, *Spiderweb*, *The Photograph*, *Making It Up*, *Consequences* and *Family Album*.

BETH LYNCH grew up in rural East Sussex, before moving to Cambridge to study and, then, lecture. She then qualified as a garden designer before moving unexpectedly to Switzerland, where she has lived (and gardened) for several years. She is the author of *Where the Hornbeam Grows*, a memoir about inheritance, loneliness and the healing power of gardening.

PROFESSOR FRANK McDONOUGH is an internationally renowned expert on the Third Reich whose many critically acclaimed works include *The Gestapo*, *Hitler and the Rise of the Nazi Party*, and *The British Empire 1815–1914*.

SUE MACGREGOR is a BBC radio broadcaster perhaps best known as a former presenter of *Woman's Hour* and the *Today* programme and the current presenter of *The Reunion*.

RICHARD MABEY is the father of modern nature writing in the UK. Since 1972 he has written some forty influential books, including the prize-winning *Nature Cure*, *Gilbert White: A Biography* and *Flora Britannica*. He is a Fellow of the Royal Society of Literature and Vice-President of the Open Spaces Society.

IAN MARTIN is an Emmy award-winning comedy writer. His TV credits include *Avenue 5*, *The Thick of It* and *Veep*. He co-wrote the BAFTA-nominated film *The Death of Stalin*. His radio comedy drama *The Hartlepool Spy* was broadcast on Christmas Day 2018 by Radio 4. He has written for the *Guardian*, *the New Statesman* and the *Architects' Journal* and has published several books, including *The Coalition Chronicles* and *Epic Space*.

JONATHAN MEADES has written and performed in some sixty television essays on topography, architecture and politics. He is the author of three works of fiction and several collections of journalism. He lives in Marseille.

ANDREW MILLER has lived in Spain, Japan, Ireland and France. His first novel, *Ingenious Pain*, won the James Tait Black Memorial Prize for Fiction, the International IMPAC Dublin Literary Award and the Grinzane Cavour prize in Italy. He has since written seven novels: *Casanova*, *Oxygen*, *The Optimists*, *One Morning Like a Bird*, *Pure*, winner of the Costa Book of the Year award 2011, *The Crossing* and *Now We Shall Be Entirely Free*.

DEBORAH MOGGACH is a BAFTA-nominated screenwriter and bestselling author. Her most recent novel is *The Carer*, and her others include *The Ex-Wives*, *Tulip Fever*, *Heartbreak Hotel* and

These Foolish Things, which was adapted into the award-winning film *The Best Exotic Marigold Hotel*.

BEN MOOR is an actor, writer and comedian. Three of his shows were collected as short stories in the book *More Trees to Climb*. In 2006 he appeared in Lasse Hallstrom's movie of *Casanova*, alongside Heath Ledger, Sienna Miller and Jeremy Irons. TV appearances include *Knowing Me, Knowing You* and *The IT Crowd*. Among his numerous radio credits, he wrote and acted in two series of the BBC sci-fi comedy *Undone*.

ALAN MOORE is widely regarded as the best and most influential writer in the history of comics. His seminal works include *Miracleman* and *Watchmen*, for which he won the coveted Hugo Award. Never one to limit himself in form or content, Moore has also published novels, *Voice of the Fire* and *Jerusalem*, and an epic poem, *The Mirror of Love*.

PAUL MORLEY grew up in Stockport, Cheshire, and has worked as a music journalist, pop svengali and broadcaster. A founder member of Art of Noise, he has written books about suicide, Joy Division, the Bakerloo line, the history of pop, the North of England, Michael Jackson and David Bowie. He collaborated with Grace Jones on her autobiography *I'll Never Write My Memoirs* and his biography of Anthony H. Wilson will be published in 2020.

JACKIE MORRIS is a children's author and artist. She has created over forty books, including beloved classics such as *Song of the Golden Hare, Tell Me a Dragon, East of the Sun, West of the Moon* and *The Wild Swans*. She has collaborated with Ted

Hughes and with Robert MacFarlane on the award-winning *The Lost Words*.

CHARLES NICHOLL is a historian, biographer and travel writer. His books include *The Reckoning* (winner of the James Tait Black prize for biography and the Crime Writers' Association 'Gold Dagger' award for non-fiction), *Somebody Else: Arthur Rimbaud in Africa* (winner of the Hawthornden Prize), and the highly acclaimed biographies *Leonardo da Vinci: The Flights of the Mind* and *The Lodger: Shakespeare on Silver Street*.

OKECHUKWU NZELU is a writer and teacher. He has written for The Wellcome Trust, *Agenda*, *PN Review*, *E-magazine* and *The Literateur*, and his essay 'Troubles with God' was published in the anthology *Safe: On Black British Men Reclaiming Space*. His radio play, *Me and Alan*, was broadcast by Roundhouse Radio, and his recently published debut novel *The Private Joys of Nnenna Maloney* has already won a New Writing North Award.

IRENOSEN OKOJIE is a Nigerian British author whose work combines the surreal and the mundane to create vivid narratives that play with form and language. Her debut novel *Butterfly Fish* and her short story collection *Speak Gigantular* have won and been shortlisted for multiple awards. A fellow of the Royal Society of Literature, Irenosen lives in east London.

RICHARD OVERY has written and edited more than thirty books, including *Why the Allies Won*, *Russia's War*, *The Morbid Age*, and *1939*. He is professor of history at the University of Exeter.

ONJALI Q. RAÚF is the founder of Making Herstory, an organisation mobilising men, women and children from all walks of life to tackle the abuse and trafficking of women and girls in the UK and beyond. In her spare time she delivers emergency aid convoys for refugee families surviving in Calais and Dunkirk, leading to the creation of O's Refugee Aid Team. She is the author of the widely acclaimed bestseller, *The Boy at the Back of the Class*.

CATHY RENTZENBRINK lives in Cornwall where she works as a writer and journalist. She is the author of the *Sunday Times* bestselling memoir *The Last Act of Love*, which was shortlisted for the Wellcome Book Prize. She has an Irish father, a Dutch husband, and will always consider herself a European.

CHRIS RIDDELL, the 2015–17 UK Waterstones Children's Laureate, is an accomplished artist, author and the political cartoonist for the *Observer*. He has enjoyed great acclaim for his books for children and has won a number of major prizes, including winning the CILIP Kate Greenaway Medal an unprecedented three times. *Goth Girl and the Ghost of a Mouse* won the Costa Children's Book Award in 2013.

ADAM ROBERTS is a science-fiction writer as well as professor of nineteenth-century literature in English at Royal Holloway, University of London. He is the author of sixteen SF novels, including *New Model Army*, *The Thing Itself* and *Jack Glass*, which won the BSFA and Campbell awards. He is also the author of various works of literary criticism and review.

Sir Tony Robinson presented twenty seasons of Channel 4's archaeology series *Time Team*, and played Baldrick in Blackadder. He wrote the BBC's *Maid Marian and Her Merry Men*, in which he played the Sheriff of Nottingham, made two series of *The Worst Jobs in History*, three series of *Walking Through History*, and an acclaimed documentary about the elderly entitled *Me and My Mum*. Also for television, he's ridden the world by train, walked the Thames, travelled coast to coast and explored the history of Australia. He has made TV documentaries on everything from *The Da Vinci Code* to the British legal system, by way of the Peasants' Revolt, the Roman Emperors, Macbeth, the Blitz and Ancient Egypt. As a children's scriptwriter he has won two RTS awards, a BAFTA and the International Prix Jeunesse. He has written thirty children's books as well as books for adults, including his autobiography *No Cunning Plan*. He has been an ambassador for the Alzheimer's Society since 2008, and received a knighthood in the Queen's Birthday Honours.

Lee Rourke is the author of the novels *Glitch, Vulgar Things,* and *The Canal* and the poetry collections *Varroa Destructor* and *Vanta Black*.

J.K. Rowling is best-known as the author of the seven Harry Potter novels, which were made into eight blockbuster films. She is also the author of *The Casual Vacancy*, a standalone novel for adults and, under the pseudonym Robert Galbraith, writes the Cormoran Strike crime novels. In 2016, she collaborated with playwright Jack Thorne and director John Tiffany on a stage play, *Harry Potter and the Cursed Child*, which is now playing in London, New York and Melbourne. In the same year, she made her debut as a screenwriter with the film *Fantastic Beasts and Where to Find Them*. Her second screenplay, *Fantastic Beasts: The Crimes of Grindelwald*, was released in 2018. As well as receiving an OBE and Companion of Honour for services to children's literature, J.K. Rowling has received many awards and honours, including: France's Légion d'Honneur; Spain's Prince of Asturias Award and Denmark's Hans Christian Andersen Award.

SOPHIE SABBAGE is an author, speaker, psychologist and patient activist whose first book, *The Cancer Whisperer*, confirmed her as an authority on how to thrive in adversity. Before her terminal cancer diagnosis in 2014, she led an award-winning business consultancy that helped leading brands respond creatively to changing winds. For thirty years she has taught thousands of people to bring their best response to their most challenging 'life-shocks', the title of her second book. She continues to offer talks and masterclasses while living with her disease and raising her daughter. She has also been to the north and south poles of her resourcefulness to stay alive.

RHIK SAMADDER is a writer, actor and broadcaster. He has a regular column with the *Guardian* and created their cult 'Inspect a Gadget' feature. He has written for the *Observer*, *Men's Health* and *Prospect* magazine, as well as being a guest, presenter and host on various radio shows. Rhik studied acting at Drama Centre London and appeared on HBO, BBC, ITV, C4 (credits including *Coronation Street*, *Emmerdale* and *Doctors*) as well as a lead role with the RSC. His first book, a memoir, is called *I never said I loved you* and is out now.

MARCUS SEDGWICK is the winner of many prizes, most notably the 2014 Michael L. Printz Award for his novel *Midwinterblood*. He has also received two Printz Honors, for *Revolver* in 2011 and *The Ghosts of Heaven* in 2016, giving him the most citations to date for America's most prestigious book prize for writing for young adults.

GENERAL SIR RICHARD SHIRREFF commissioned into the British Army as a cavalry officer after reading History at Oxford. In his thirty-seven years of service he commanded soldiers on operations from the most junior to the most senior levels. He saw combat as a tank commander in the First Gulf War, experienced many of the complexities of Northern Ireland during his three tours there and learned first-hand the challenges of bringing peace to the Balkans in both Kosovo and Bosnia. He returned to Iraq as a multinational commander in 2006–7. His last seven years in uniform were spent in two senior NATO command posts: Commander of the Allied Rapid Reaction Corps and Deputy Supreme Allied Commander Europe; the Alliance's deputy strategic commander and the most senior British general in the Alliance. He is the author of the bestselling novel *War With Russia*.

PETER STANFORD is an award-winning journalist, writer and broadcaster. A former editor of the *Catholic Herald*, his explorations of the history, theology and cultural significance of religious ideas include *The Devil: A Biography*, *Martin Luther: Catholic Dissident*, and *Angels: A Visible and Invisible History*.

Isy Suttie is a comedian, actress and writer who started performing stand-up in 2002. Her first book, a memoir, was called *The Actual One* and she has written for the *Guardian*, the *Observer* and *Glamour*. She is a regular writer and performer on BBC Radio 4, where her show *Pearl and Dave* won a Gold Sony Award in 2013. Her TV acting credits include Dobby in *Peep Show* and Esther in *Shameless*, and she has been nominated for three British Comedy Awards.

Sandi Toksvig, OBE, was born in Copenhagen, Denmark and brought up in Europe, Africa and the United States. She began her comedy career at Cambridge where she wrote and performed in the first all-woman Footlights show. Sandi is well known to UK audiences as a broadcaster, including celebrated series such as *Call My Bluff*, *QI*, the *News Quiz* and the *Great British Bake Off*. Author of more than twenty fiction and non-fiction books for children and adults, Sandi is president of the Writers' Guild of Great Britain as well as an activist for gender equality. In 2014 she co-founded the Women's Equality Party. 'Fred' is the Danish word for peace.

Pete Townshend is the lead guitarist and principal song-writer of The Who – one of the most influential rock bands of the twentieth century, selling over 100 million records world-wide – and the composer of the rock operas *Tommy* and *Quadrophenia*. His autobiography *Who I Am* was published in 2012 and his first novel, *The Age of Anxiety*, will be published in November 2019.

COLIN TUDGE is a biologist by education and a writer by trade, who worked for some years for the *New Scientist* and then BBC Radio 3. Mainly, he writes books, including *The Secret Life of Trees, The Variety of Life, Good Food for Everyone Forever, Why Genes are Not Selfish and People are Nice,* and, most recently, *Six Steps Back to the Land.* He is also co-founder of the Oxford Real Farming Conference and The College for Real Farming and Food Culture.

ANNA WHITELOCK's bestselling debut, *Mary Tudor: England's First Queen,* was published to critical acclaim in 2009. She is a Senior Lecturer in Early Modern History at Royal Holloway, University of London. She regularly appears on television and radio and has written for the *Guardian, BBC History,* the *Sunday Telegraph* and the *New York Times.*

KATE WILLIAMS is a social historian and broadcaster. She is the author of the widely acclaimed and bestselling novels *The Storms of War* and *The Edge of the Fall* and four historical biographies of Emma Hamilton, Queen Victoria, Elizabeth II and Empress Josephine – which is being made into a major TV series. She studied for her DPhil at Oxford, is Professor of Public History at the University of Reading, and has also taught creative writing under Andrew Motion at Royal Holloway. She judges various prizes and was the Chair of the Costa Book Award.

MICHAEL WOOD has worked as a journalist, broadcaster and filmmaker, and is author of several highly acclaimed and best-selling books, including *Domesday, In Search of the Dark Ages, Legacy, In Search of the Trojan War,* and *In Search of England.* He has over a hundred documentary films to his name, among them *Legacy*, *The Story of India* and *In the Footsteps of Alexander the Great*, for which he also wrote the accompanying book.

LOUISA YOUNG is the author of many books, including the best-selling *My Dear I Wanted to Tell You*, which was shortlisted for the Costa Novel Award, and the *Lionboy* series, co-written with her daughter. Her most recent book is a memoir, *You Left Early: A True Story of Love and Alcohol*.

ACKNOWLEDGEMENTS

The publishers thank Sophie Lazar for her invaluable contribution, including thinking of contributors, approaching them and editing all the contributions. This book could not have been put together, especially in such a short time, without her.

The phrase 'The love you take' is taken from Lennon and McCartney's 'The End', which is copyright © Sony/ATV Music Publishing LLC

A NEW EUROPEAN SONG by Mary Beard was written in 2016 for BBC Radio 4's *A Point of View* and includes lyrics from Pink Floyd's 'Time', which are copyright © BMG Rights Management

LIKE A PFUCKKING TAART! by Holly Johnson includes lyrics from George and Ira Gershwin's 'I got rhythm', which are copyright © Warner Chappell Music, Inc

POLYPHONY by Richard Mabey includes a short quote from *Granite Island: A Portrait of Corsica* (1971) by Dorothy Carrington, published by Penguin Classics, and another from *Ayre* (2004) by Osvaldo Golijov, published by Boosey & Hawkes.

ON THE PLAYING FIELDS OF FIESOLE by James Hanning quotes from the speech Boris Johnson gave at the Conservative conference in Birmingham on 3 October 2016.

A THEORY OF LIGHT by Hugh Aldersey-Williams is adapted from a text prepared in association with Katie Paterson's *First There is a Mountain* . . .

THE BREXIT POEM was compiled from statements made by Alan Moore, then edited and approved by him.